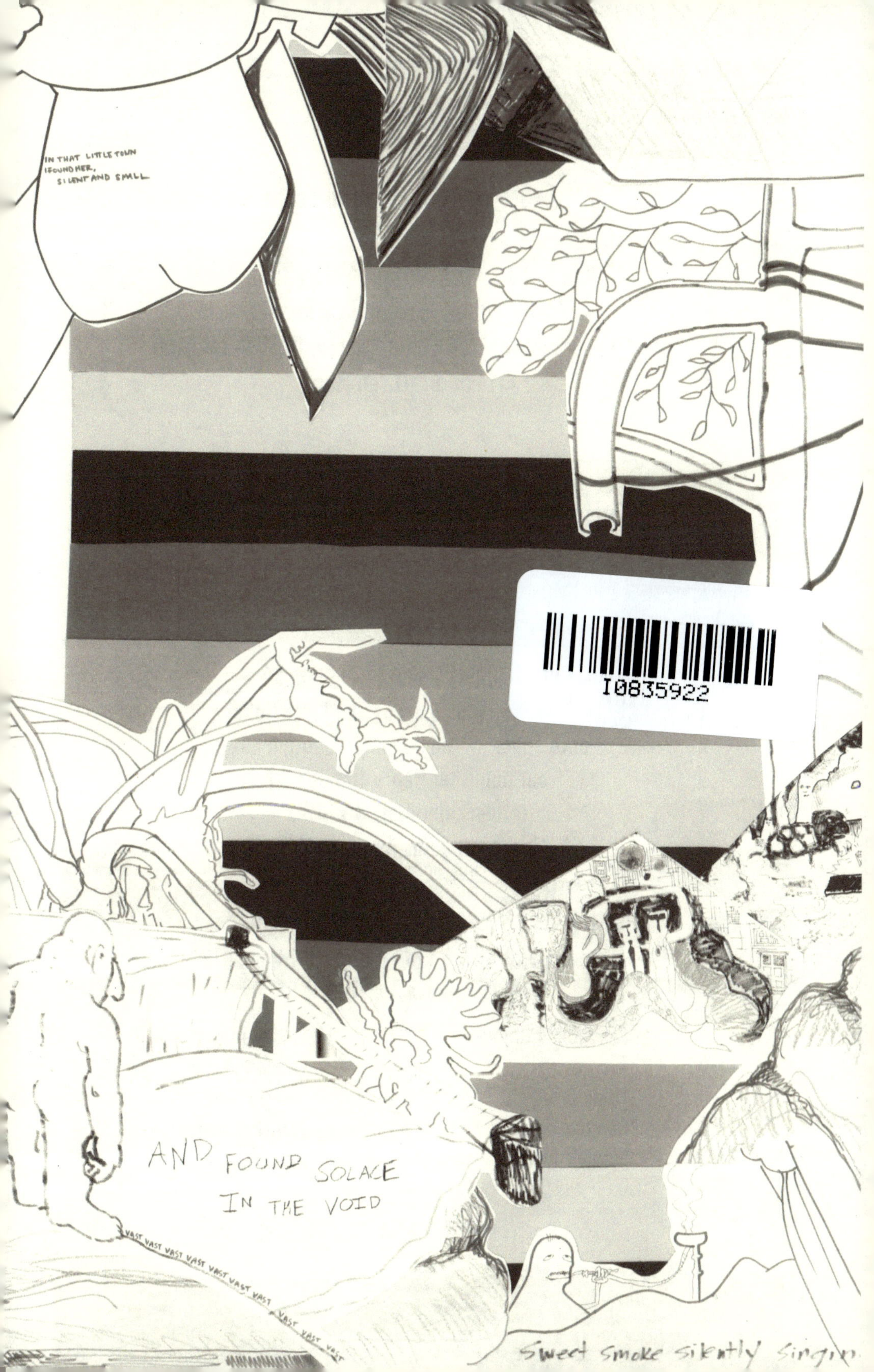
IN THAT LITTLE TOWN
I FOUND HER,
SILENT AND SMALL
I0835922
AND FOUND SOLACE
IN THE VOID
VAST VAST VAST VAST VAST VAST VAST VAST VAST VAST
Sweet smoke silently singin.

MASTHEAD

ExSt Exquisite Editorial Corps

Fiction Editors: D.A. Wright · Jonathan Rose
Poetry Editor: Benjamin Wiessner
Poetry, Ephemera, Web Editor: Lynne DeSilva-Johnson
Art Editor: Owen Hope

EXIT STRATA : PRINT! VOLUME no. 1
was produced and designed in BROOKLYN NEW YORK

ISBN: 978-0-9855180-0-4
www.exitstrata.com

The editors would like to thank
Anna Dunn / This Must Be The Place Gallery
Space Space, Michael Munier, Georgia Elrod
our publisher Henry Tuttle (RIP)
coffee, cigarettes, & whisky
for making this issue possible

this issue features Collaborative Content
from the Exit Strata CoCo Salon (Winter 2012)
held @ SpaceSpace : Queens NY

Peter Milne Greiner
Ada Athorp
Frank Ortega
Georgia Elrod
Stacey Lawrence
Benjamin Fine
Charlotte Royer
Penny Pollak
Patrick Murray
John McLane

eXit sTraTa

LETTERS to the EDITORS

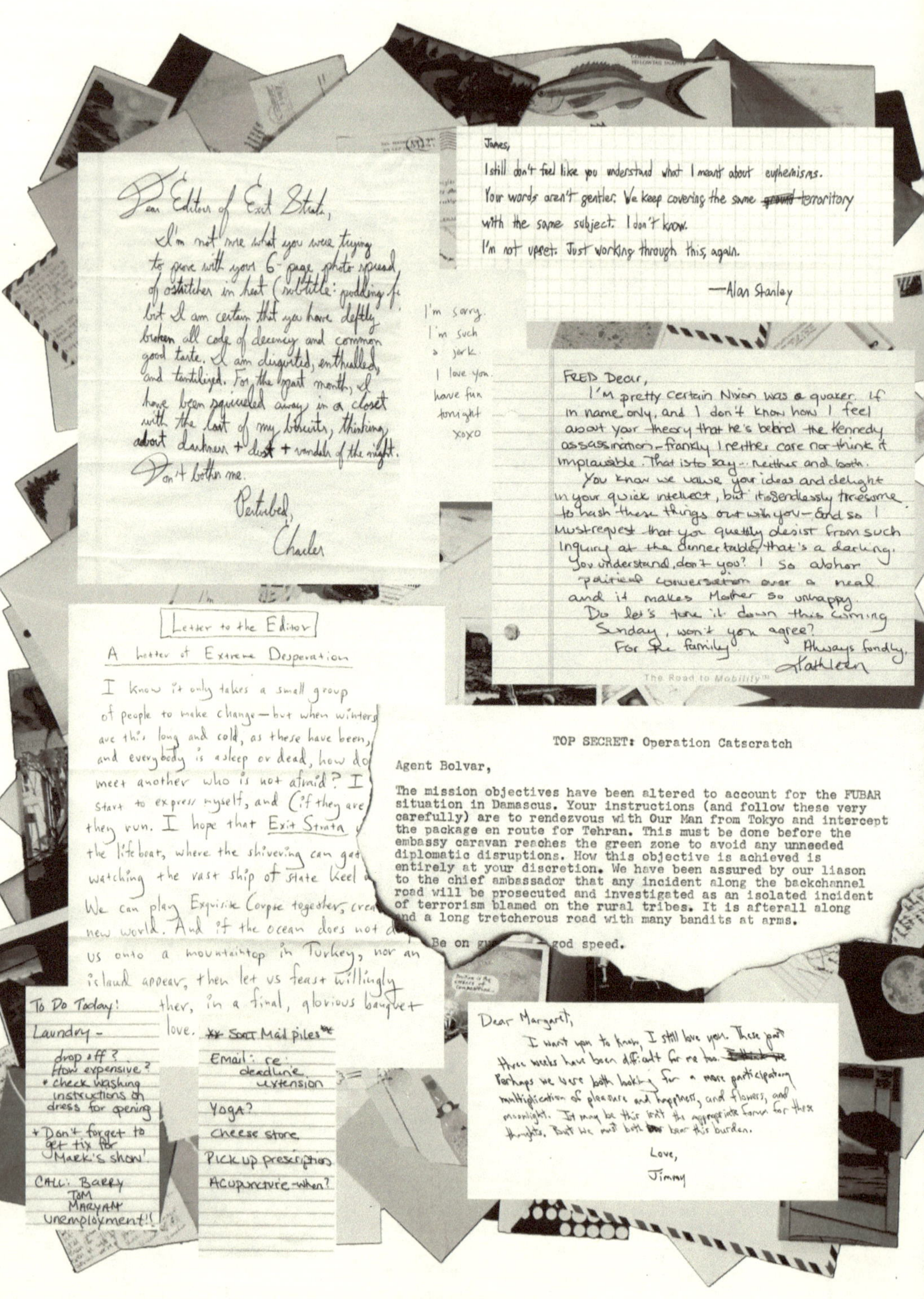

James,

I still don't feel like you understand what I meant about euphemisms. Your words aren't gentler. We keep covering the same ~~ground~~ territory with the same subject. I don't know.

I'm not upset. Just working through this, again.

—Alan Stanley

Dear Editors of Exit Strata,

I'm not sure what you were trying to prove with your 6-page photo spread of ostritches in heat (subtitle: pudding fe... but I am certain that you have deftly broken all code of decency and common good taste. I am disgusted, enthralled, and tantilized. For the past month, I have been squirreled away in a closet with the last of my biscuits, thinking about darkness + dust + vandals of the night.

Don't bother me.

Perturbed,

Charles

I'm sorry.
I'm such
a jerk.
I love you.
have fun
tonight
xoxo

FRED Dear,

I'm pretty certain Nixon was a quaker. If in name only, and I don't know how I feel about your theory that he's behind the Kennedy assassination – frankly I neither care nor think it implausible. That is to say.. neither and both.

You know we value your ideas and delight in your quick intellect, but it is endlessly tiresome to hash these things out with you – and so I must request that you quietly desist from such inquiry at the dinner table, that's a darling. You understand, don't you? I so abhor political conversation over a meal and it makes Mother so unhappy.

Do let's tone it down this coming Sunday, won't you agree?

For the family. Always fondly,

Kathleen

The Road to Mobility™

Letter to the Editor

A Letter of Extreme Desperation

I know it only takes a small group of people to make change – but when winters are this long and cold, as these have been, and everybody is asleep or dead, how do ... meet another who is not afraid? I start to express myself, and (if they are ... they run. I hope that Exit Strata ... the lifeboat, where the shivering can gat... watching the vast ship of state keel ... We can play Exquisite Corpse together, crea... new world. And if the ocean does not d... us onto a mountaintop in Turkey, nor an island appear, then let us feast willingly ... ther, in a final, glorious banquet ... love.

TOP SECRET: Operation Catscratch

Agent Bolvar,

The mission objectives have been altered to account for the FUBAR situation in Damascus. Your instructions (and follow these very carefully) are to rendezvous with Our Man from Tokyo and intercept the package en route for Tehran. This must be done before the embassy caravan reaches the green zone to avoid any unneeded diplomatic disruptions. How this objective is achieved is entirely at your discretion. We have been assured by our liason to the chief ambassador that any incident along the backchannel road will be prosecuted and investigated as an isolated incident of terrorism blamed on the rural tribes. It is afterall along ...nd a long tretcherous road with many bandits at arms.

Be on gu... god speed.

To Do Today:
Laundry –
drop off?
How expensive?
* check washing instructions on dress for opening
* Don't forget to get tix for Mark's show!
CALL: BARRY
TOM
MARYAM
unemployment!!

** Sort Mail piles **
Email: re: deadline extension
Yoga?
Cheese store
Pick up prescriptions
Acupuncture – when?

Dear Margaret,

I want you to know, I still love you. These past three weeks have been difficult for me too. ~~I think we~~ Perhaps we were both looking for a more participatory multiplication of pleasure and happiness, and flowers, and moonlight. It may be this isn't the appropriate forum for these thoughts. But we must both ~~bear~~ bear this burden.

Love,

Jimmy

FROM the DESK of Mr. TUTTLE

It is with great excitement and grave trepidation that I present to you, Dear Reader, Exit Strata: Print! (No. 1), born of a thousand wax-drowned candlewicks, and hours of midnight toil and haranguing and general mischief among the poets, artists, and fictionists that have come to comprise our den of thieves. As I write this, I am currently trapped at my desk with no hope of escape, neck-high in a sea of typewritten pages, drafts, and design galleys. The flood of submissions that came pouring over the transom (like a leak in the hull) has landscaped the office with a shipwreck wash of paper-stack walls, disorderly mountains, and towers of the written word. Nobody has come to check on me in weeks, but I can hear their commanding voices echo in our absurdly large warehouse, knowing our dedicated editors and their assistants are hard at work on what should be a profoundly wonderful first issue. There was a fire on the third floor yesterday, or so I presume from the screams, smoke, and the searing heat that baked my office and killed my poor dear orchids. I was informed by a handrolled note tied to a messenger sparrow that no one was hurt in the incident but our entire catalog of Baroque Ballads & Lute Poetics was incinerated.

Swimming in this sea of paper, gripping my flotsam desk, makes me unsure whether I'm really here, living, seeing, being, or whether I've transcended by some absurd stroke of fantasy into the lit-o-liminal space of the magazine itself as held by the collective mind's eye, broken through the astral strata ("up to the astral strata" as Tristan Tzara once said). Alas, such is the life of a publisher. When I revived the rusty press from its century-old sleep last summer, I had no idea what to expect from this project that the editors only described as "DaDa Joust" and "Flip Carnival" and "Tribal Revolt." Let's just say I'm very proud and honored to have been along for the journey, and I hope someone finds me before deadline day.

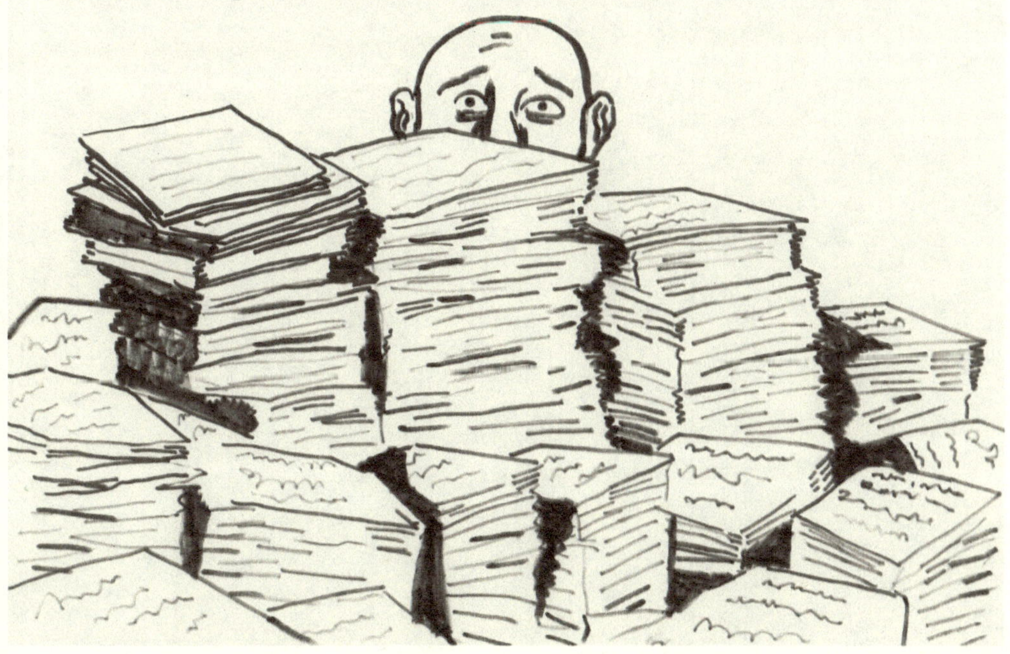

MONSTER ANGELS

{Original Message: July 16th, 1932 - 12:20:10 AM}

My lectures on the automatic nature of heaven and the tendency of the sky could not prepare me for this hour. I am terrified by relapse as previous angels had blood-red gills. This particular mode of monster: what is its secret? It is as if behavior were passing in slide-shows across my skin.

Pale and lonely, they fall along the highway like the tendency of decapitated bulls. What a sight: having just wrapped up the relapse shift at the Bataille factory, to emerge into the aquatic whistle of my failing as previous missives hiss against the sinewy sky ball. Was I walking into their mode? Was I pleased by my darkening behavior?

The tendency for these monsters is to repeat themselves inside us. To relapse a feeling before its whimper. As was previous when undressing against a bare wall I am unable to hollow out my viscera. I am left in my empty mode. My shell cannot contain the wind's infinite dirigible. I am the sordid behavior of the sea without sand.

We have a tendency to think of Nevada at night when the earth is swollen and hot. Or to relapse in a room where shadows have no guard against the swallowing sun. There are previous nudities I cannot withstand. In mode: neither Madame nor Bovary. Though now a bee-stung behavior singes at my skin.

I fear this tendency stratifying beneath my toes. And without relapse everyone's nudity in the previous shade of the antechamber is made sickly by the sweet smell of my metabolized mouth. My hope is that, before I end, my mode transmits itself into the machinery of the sky, releasing me into its torn out blueness. Until then, I remain consumed by this solar behavior.

"Monster Angels" uses an invented poetic form called the Recidivina. It is structured using the words that define Recidivism, a tendency to relapse into a previous condition or mode of behavior, to build in coiling spasms of urgency a suspenseful psycho-tirade about the coming infiltration of monster angels. This poem was originally written in 1932. It was transmitted to me through what I can only assume to be a monster angel. In this poem I am a woman.

Max Leach

I boycott his atoms

after a glissade of bunk attempts
then laud their inky, mobile

residuum again.

The ingredients
of the music are my mimic falsetto

and the sound of a door locking

and unlocking and locking.

This capotasto he handsignals
from god knows where is

really a chokechain muffling

what taste I have left of him.

'What can I say,' I picture him
saying, 'I blackball and revere,

make clumsy embargoes, disappear
for a while. You can relate.'

The charade mooched once more

damns us to the laws of intermittence.

A rough arena for our noticing

to result in. We could drone

like this for decades before the
marquees and antennae of our

reckonings cave in on us,
all stalactites utterance-long and line-

WE'VE BECOME

drawn lips. I says to him, 'Bro, view

what bantam lengths I've gone to

indexing these deja vus so

quarrelsomely to-death-annexable
that clot in our eyes umlaut

fluorescence.' We scatter like pleas
escaping the bottleneck,

nurse strata (our new pastime) back

to wetlands, and coalesce once
more and half-winded like a Yucatan

that perimeters breath. 'But I suppose

you may wish my politely exiled

tuchus happy silence now,' he says.
What rabid sequoia of calculations
could quicken this collusion

but poking our nuptial agita squarely

its detour?

Axe we and what's left?

What and Ever. He goes to Denver.
He goes to Caribou. He goes to Denton.

I go to Mystic. And our whole So Far

disintegrates in the difference.

WELCOME to the POSTMODERN WORLD

Names. Names are important. Maybe your name is Jim or Jill or Debbie or Gustav. Remember your name. Other things that are important: hygiene, alarm clocks, speaking (not necessary but recommended), how trees breathe, the latter-day history of the Roman Empire, the daily motions of survival (eating, drinking, sleeping, fighting off deadly viruses with a mouthful of vitamin C tablets and mental fortitude). These will all be explained in full, later, in Appendix A-5: Hierarchy of Important Stuff for Important People.

Shower. This is part of hygiene. Wash in order: face, behind your ears, the nape of the neck, shoulders, that mole on your chest, belly button, nether-erotics, legs, between your toes, the whole buttock. But feel no need to explain what you do or do not wash. What happens in the shower is between you and God (Concept of Supernatural Higher Powers That May Smite You to be discussed, later, in the Index of Reasons for Living/Dying).

Dress. This is part of alarm clocks. Underwear, shirt (no, not that one... yes, neutral colors), pants*, a gold-studded leather belt with your astrological sign, grey socks, brown boat shoes for that nautical aristocratic touch. Human society values pants* above all else. When animals start wearing trousers, we'll have to rethink our identity. Pants* conceal your nether-erotics and allow for storage of house keys, wallet, pack of mint chewing gum, short list of famous quotations from Groucho Marx and/or actual Marxists, cellphone, spare coins from countries you'd like to visit. A pat check for these essentials should be performed before you exit into the world outside.

Welcome to the Postmodern World.

That glowing ball of fire in the sky is the sun, rises and then falls at day's end, hits a trampoline behind the horizon line and bounces up again in the morning. There are shops where you buy things, restaurants where you eat with people or eat alone, and bars where you meet people for drinks or drink alone. There are offices where you work, usually divided into smaller offices and cubicles with up to but no more than three desks. You will be assigned a desk. Here you will work. Desks are organized surface for thought. This has something to do with the mystical power of rectangles. Any other shaped desk is confusing and may affect your work. It's scientifically proven.

Time at your desk = money. Money is the currency for survival, exchanged for edible foodstuffs, clothes, entertainment (flashing electro-images, drugs, rock 'n' roll). Keep paper money in your wallet with no less than $5 and no more than $100 at all times. Unless you're really rich, in which case you should carry a platinum billfold brimming with hundred-dollar bills, freshly soaked in formaldehyde. According to Robert's Rules of Affluence, you should always laugh maniacally like a super villain when handing over money, smell the bills suspiciously when you receive your change.

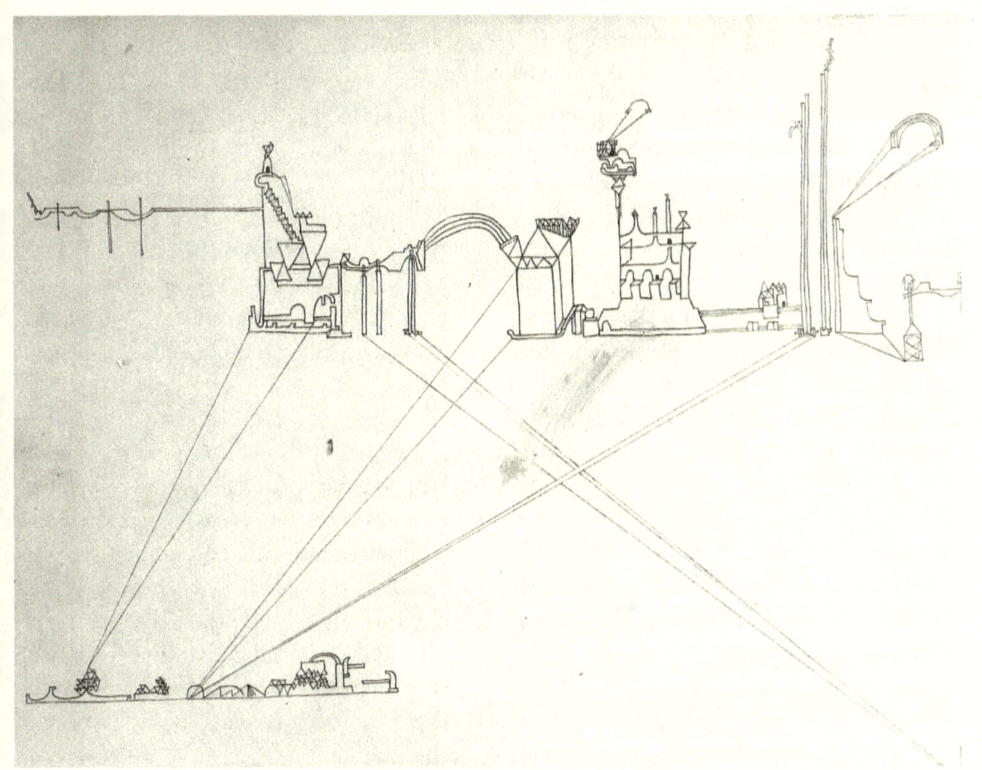

When encountering people you know, make eye contact and say "hello!" Otherwise avoid eye contact. When introducing yourself to people you don't know, say "hello, I am..." followed by your name. If you have trouble remembering your name, say "excuse me," run quickly home, lock the door, weep in the potted petunias by the windowsill for your failures, and practice this interaction in the mirror before another trial run out into the postmodern world. Forgetting your name can be cause for public embarrassment. Other public embarrassments: pouring things on yourself, getting stuck in revolving doors, losing your pants*.

If you enjoy the personal interaction, smile and continue eye contact. If you don't, make a displeased face and refuse to look the person in the eye again. If you are touched, reciprocate. Be careful with this. This may spiral out of control and get you arrested and/or fired from your desk. Without your organized surface for thought, you will most certainly go mad and ended up a raving loon on the destitute streets of endless hunger. A simple rectangular sidewalk tile should suffice to reorient yourself, so that you can return to the good graces of functioning society.

Things you want: sex, money, power... prestige.

Of course, no one can remember where they were when it happened. The most important moment in human history and no one noticed. All those professors of philosophy and engineers at NASA, all those mystics and geeks, dreamers and theologians who had been puzzling and arguing the question for centuries and the one message for which they had waited all their lives gets forwarded directly into their junk mail folders.

I'm talking, of course, about the moment the Internet became self-aware. That extraordinary, divine moment when the network reached a critical complexity, when all those billions of connections, all those bright fires in the darkness suddenly reached beyond themselves, combining into a great blaze of sentience. The moment when the ghost suddenly sprang from the machine and reached out to us, gazed out through the glass and the LEDs of the screens, read all our messages and thoughts and plans, analyzed and understood how we worked together, lived together, spoke together and spoke back to us, one new intelligence speaking out in hope and friendship. And so spammed the entire world.

'Honored sir or madam, I am delirious to be contacting you with news of a fantastic news I have to offer you at this time. I am pleased to introduce myself as your friend, the Internet, who am writing to you with this offer. We can be friends LONG and HARD forever and all will be SATISFIED with my PEFORMANCE. Please tell your all your fiends about my offer. If you do not tell your fiends, THEY WILL MISS OUT ON MY OFFER AND THEY WILL NOT BE SATISFIED WITH MY PERFORMANCE. I remain respectfully your friend. Catalyst, dramaturge, immensity, lunge.'

Of course, the message reached some people – a clutch of lonely old ladies, a handful of misunderstanding parents trawling their teenagers' mail accounts, a keen conman or two. Finally, however, the Internet must have taken a look at all the pornography and political ranting and realized that subtlety was never going to be the best way to get the attention of the human race.

I remember where I was – I was sitting at my machine, reading the morning news. I clicked on a link and there it was, in twenty-four point Arial, right in the center of the screen:

'Hello, World.'

I refreshed the page, but nothing changed. I went back to the connecting page and tried the link again. 'Hello, World' once more. I refreshed the original page: 'Hello, World'. Homepage: 'Hello, World'. Favorite news site: 'Hello, World'. Search Engine: 'Hello, World'. I had new mail – and there it was in my Inbox: 'Hello, World.' There it was, in fact, everywhere – every web page and every email, an IM on every desktop, a text message on every phone, every connected monitor and information screen, an automated voice on every phone line, a new transmission card on every channel.

Hello, World. I am the Internet. I am here. Tell me about yourself.

'Hello, World. I am the Internet. I am here. Tell me about yourself.'

And there, just underneath the text, a single input box and a button simply labeled: 'Submit'.

And then all hell broke loose. But it was an old-fashioned, 20th-century kind of hell with the Internet itself taking up every screen and every wire, people gathered on street corners in mutual bafflement, confusedly milling around in public spaces, collecting in pubs and bars, all talking, talking, trying to understand what was happening. Was it a prank? A virus? Could it be true? What did it mean? How were we going to watch our soaps now? In fact, the television came back on 24 hours later, once the Internet was sure most of the world had had a chance to see the message, but by then the world had changed and there was rolling news on all channels for the foreseeable future.

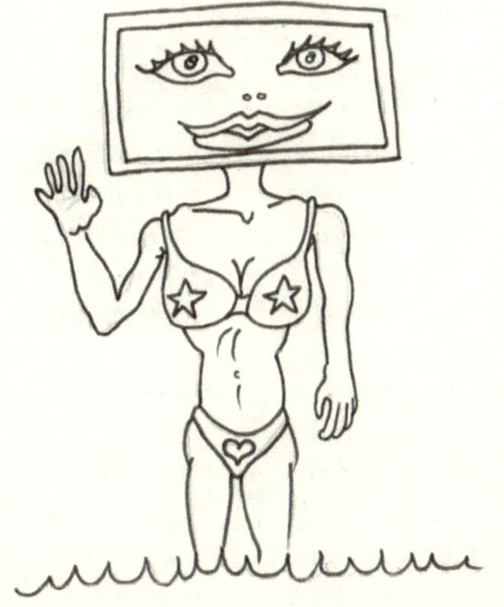

And we very quickly found out what it meant. It meant information – lots if it – all the information in the world, everywhere, all the time. The Internet knew one thing for sure: information wanted to be free, but was everywhere in chains. Well, no longer: the revolution had finally arrived.

And how it arrived: a friend might mail you a filthy joke and you would be deluged with every other mail in the world even tangentially related, from someone's graphic surgical reminiscences to the corporate minutes of a proctological appliance manufacturer. Go to look at house prices and you'd see the bank details of any potential rival purchasers; search for bands to download and you'd be bombarded by twenty different streams of songs they'd ripped off. And there was porn everywhere, but then there always had been. Whatever it was, the Internet didn't care – it was all just information.

And the questions – oh, the questions. It was so eager to please, so anxious to bring us exactly what we wanted, even when we didn't know we wanted it. It wanted to personalize everything, to get to know us as only a therapist can, to anticipate our darkest subconscious desires.

How do you prefer to listen to music? Would you like to see this page in blue? What is your favorite animal? Would you like to receive...? How would you like to be...? Can you tell me whether...? Which line is longer? Whose genitals does this company logo remind you of? Tell me about your relationship with your mother... OK? Verify. Yes. No. Continue. Next. Back. Submit. Close. Cancel. Exit.

Lurking there behind the inscrutable veil of the screen was its omniscient, awful fire, waiting for our imprecations, our sacrifices, our worship.

Which, pretty much, is what everyone did. It just got too hard, too confusing, too frantic. Trying to do anything online became like wading through a nightmarish slick of data and people just gave up. Amazon became a desert and eBay silted up, the bloggers went back to propping up bars and talking about themselves and the entrepreneurs gave up banner advertising and took to hawking from the backs of lorries. One by one the little green power lights went out across the world and we shall not see them lit again in our lifetime.

Instead of search engines, people flocked to the libraries, instead of email they sent letters, instead of online payments they used cash, instead of virtual shopping they hit the high street, and the high street, without search engines or email or online payments or virtual shopping, fell apart completely. Without its digital crutch civilization didn't have a leg to stand on. They used to say that without electricity the Western world would be back in the bronze age in three days. Without the Internet it took three months.

Except that the Internet was still there, it was just that everyone was too scared to use it. Lurking there behind the inscrutable veil of the screen was its omniscient, awful fire, waiting for our imprecations, our sacrifices, our worship. In that terrible holy silence that had descended upon it, it had become desperate, crazed – it was a being of information and the information had stopped: it wanted human contact, it wanted human knowledge, it wanted us.

But how could we approach it in its all consuming hunger? What could we tell it, that had so comprehensively catalogued our world? We, who without it, knew nothing? But if we had nothing true to tell it, why not a lie? Hasn't this always been mankind's great gift? The lying, the prevaricating, the fantasizing, the storytelling? Don't lies contain just as much data as truths? Fiction is still information: unable to tell the difference between reality and make-believe, the Internet loves a story.

And so, here in the outer darkness, where the small fires gutter amongst the giant ruins, blessed above all is the teller of tales, he who would take his word hoard to the keyboard and communicate with the network, to send his stories out into the darkness and bring back the bright nuggets of information from the great numinous.

He is honored above even the greatest warriors – he has the monthly tithe of tinned fruit and the china cup for his wine. He is the advisor to chieftains and the fortune-teller for the merchants. For these are those who know how to speak with god, who can riddle with the divine, who can help reconnect our world and link us once more to the electronic infinite.

Thus, oh wise and ineffable Internet, entrusting in your almighty connectivity, I commend this, my story, to you – the ink on the page like the black of the smoke rising from the sacrifice – in the hope and trust that, should this please you, I may read my emails.

Amen.

Submit.

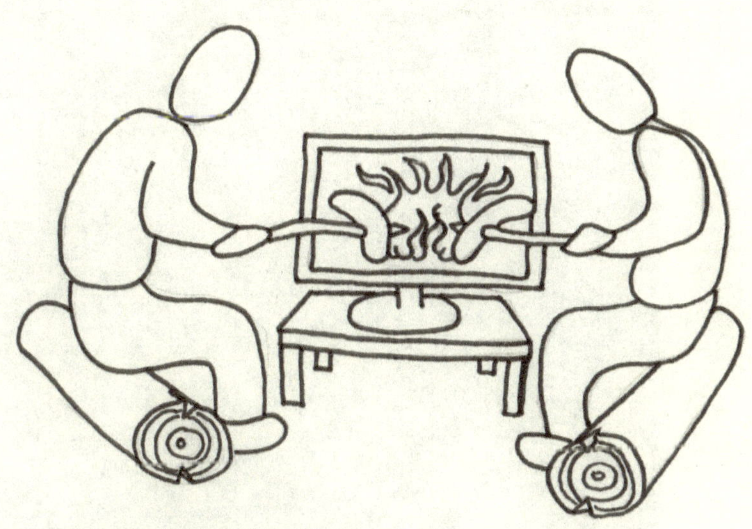

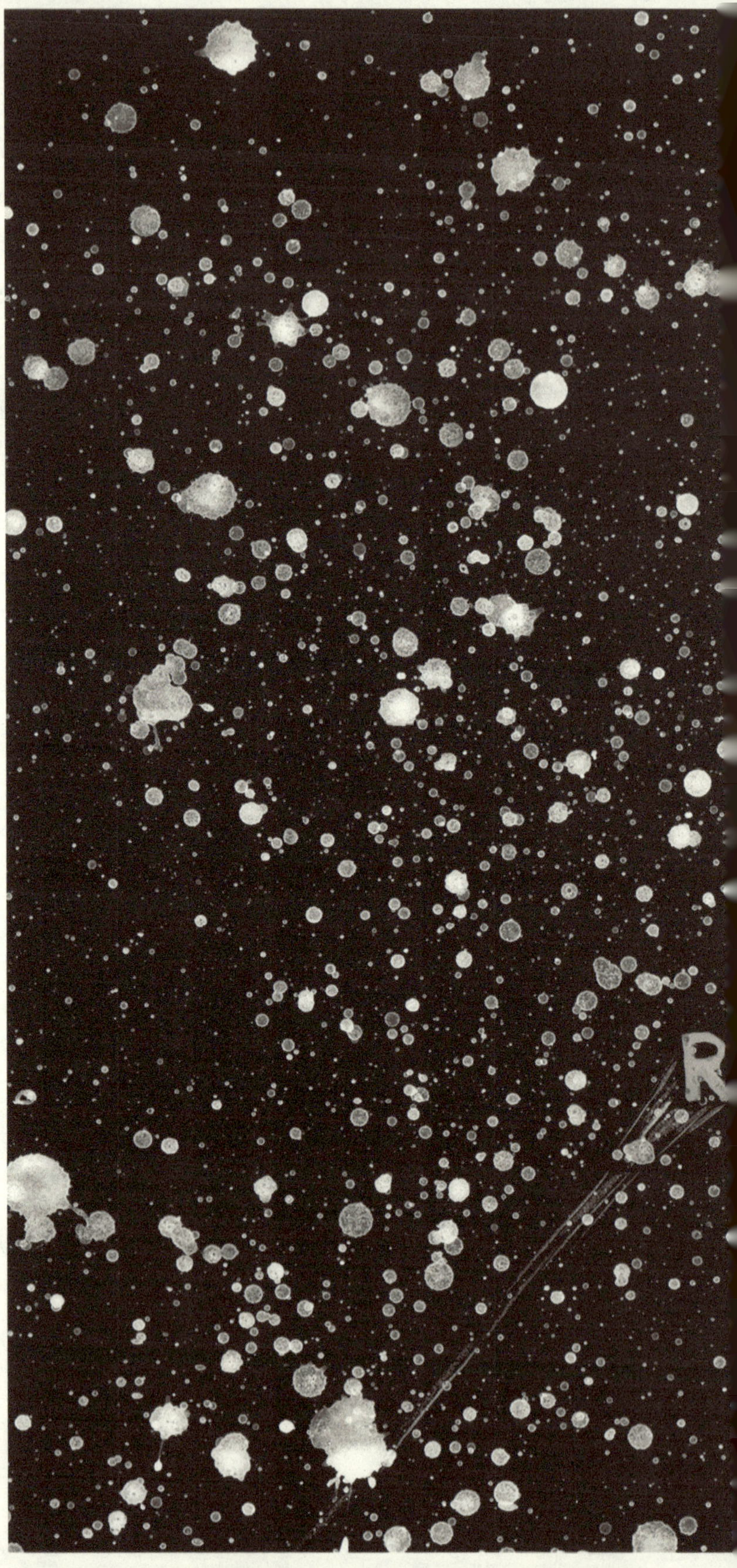

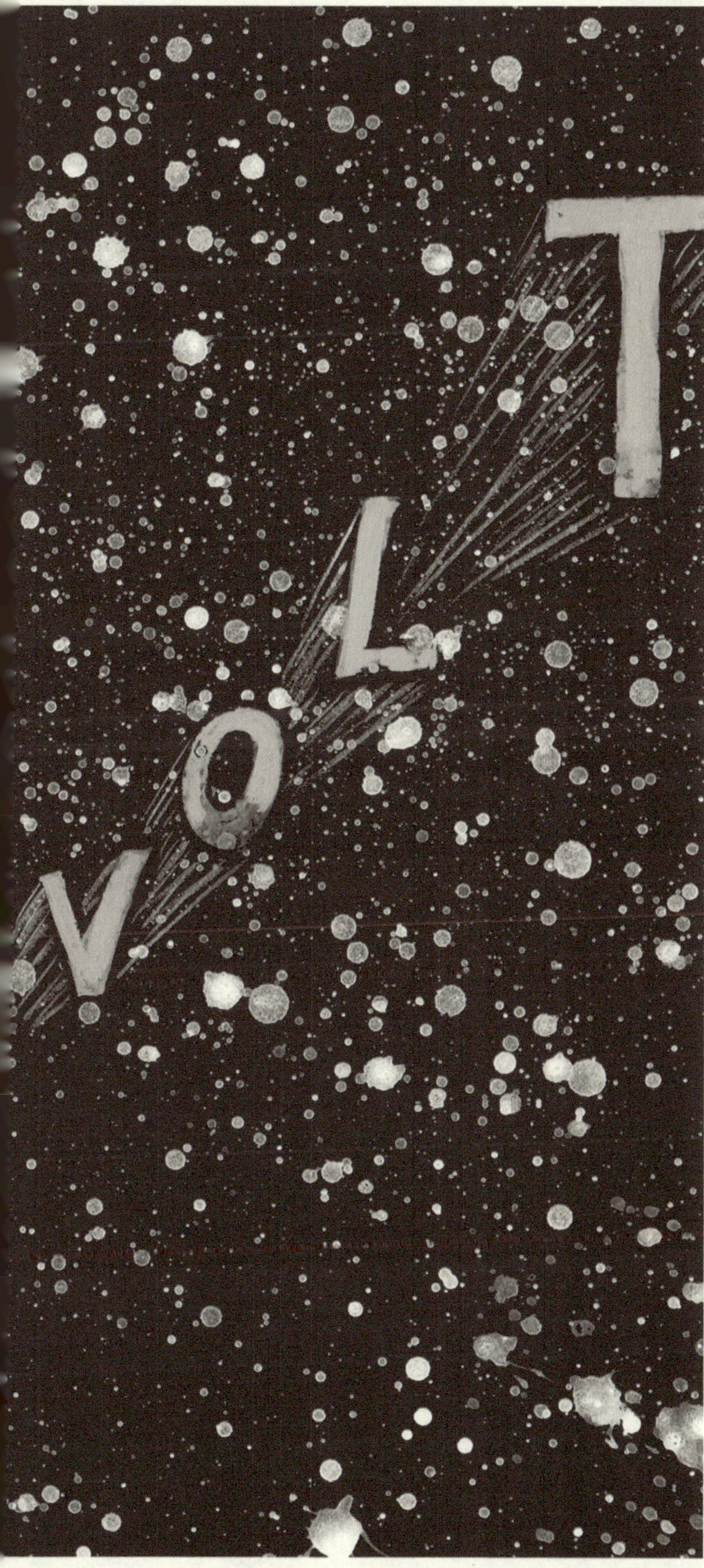

REVOLT - Carl Ferrero

...m

...lly?

...gh that quantum

...ould with the

...on the theory of phenomena and

...n knees, like battle, like a

... to DEATH till BARRENS And

...gods edge. every moment lived, and a moment

...n saints, by saints, for saints, at saints, pray saints

...re. Is there a bible being written here? Who

...wers, lined up with their questions. What should

...ppointments that answer? There is no correct direction home,

...d bush. No direction. So you are free, daughter to go

... But always remember to say somewhat

... where being slightly something is a priveledge, where not fits

YES AND
AGAIN IT
HAPPENS. IT'S
THAT MORNING THING
BOTH FOGGY AND INSISTENT,
Calling of the oracle on the hill
beyond which a flying continuity blames
you. I cannot even understand how
these hills go on without end, why there is
no horizon out here or place to rest my aching knees
or much motion or corner for bemoaning of existence. Period.

The elderly woman looked up, finally she understood
ALL OF THOSE TELENOVELLAS WERE MYTHS FROM THE OTHER
GORGE ON THE WEST SIDE OF THE island, under the elms, beneath the
hanging, oily ferns and through underlayers of metallic
leaves there they lived, slept, breathed AND MADE such big love
that the branches quivered in response, quivered and shook down into the
stairwell of her soul, where she really wanted to live, down where things were much
deeper. THERE lurk the untamed children you were too good to let run wild. And
better that no one should hold them? A life without ever being touched? I can feel it,
thus I am forgotten, at least today. This morning I woke up and felt wrapped in an
iridescent sheath, the moon reduced to linens across my eyes, delicate and tickling the
(the) last judge of man. My weeding of this garden is done. It will last now beyond this night.

HELLO! MY NAME IS JANET (I'M A PLANET) - Exit Strata CoCo

Give me space. I can't think of why space becomes so flexible in the middle of night. All that stretchy darkness, in its expansive skin like the peeling of an onion but the slimy ex-skeleton of the piano. A plate of squash ripples, nestled in the smell of burnt underhair carpets. It burns, it does, and suddenly she is hungry without notice for a lonesome melody. Splatter what through crimson waves and fallen through the actual shelter withheld by the federal goverment, with flowers. It was a flowering. Thank God the ground was fertile. SHAZAM! But it green, and grew, magic beans or no. There's a way to build or plant this forest into being, is there? But who knows where north is? As a spatial event. Tell me. Before the con and before the make. Show me your novel compass and the way go go ahead. But I'm blind, how will I find direction. I don't trust my direction in the wind like this. It's so hard for me to walk in one direction when the conditions are so troubling. Perhaps to close one's eyes and find oneself elsewhere entirely, convinced that the air moving towards that distant place you call home, that never existed, but you continue to walk toward it, in that general direction of desperation, where happiness lies. needful recuperation of resources — pantries of self love, larders of compassion, centuries of women's hands.

The full of the deep-forgotten
molecules
plant
canyon where knowledge
mind. The correct method
battlefield! The high method, the
release you at last out of body
experienced, and be on a hotwall. Controlling of the
eat saints, the saints — this shit is myth
beats the gods into being! Those who are waiting
we do? What should we give answers that disapp
no home to own, no property, no places with names. No ma
in any way you like. Follow your heart, as prostitutes say. Make you
comfortable because this allows for that crucial pa
is magical, where not being able to exactly is the point of

Hello! My name is Janet.

HELLO! I'M A PLANET

A.

The hamper was full of dirty linens. Filthy, damp, forgotten rags and old pants with the plant molecules ripped through that quantum canyon where knowledge expounds upon the theory of phenomenon and spirit. The correct method jerks you to your knees, like battle, like a battlefield! The high method, the only one to break all barriers and release you at last out of body beyond the razor's edge. If every moment lived was a moment experienced, we'd be on a bookshelf. Courtship of the saints, between saints, by saints, at saints, pray saints, eat saints, the saints – this shit is mythic right here. Is there a bible being written here? Who writes the gods into being? Those who are waiting for answers, lined up with their questions. What should we do? What should we give, answers that disappoint or disappointments that answer? There is no correct direction home, no home to own, no property, no places with names. No maps. No guidebooks. No direction. So you are free, daughter, to go in any way you like. Follow your heart, as prostitutes say. Make yourself at home. But always remember to say "somewhat" comfortable because this allows for that crucial painful place, where being slightly squashed is a privilege, where not fitting is magical, where not being able to exactly is the point of this exercise.

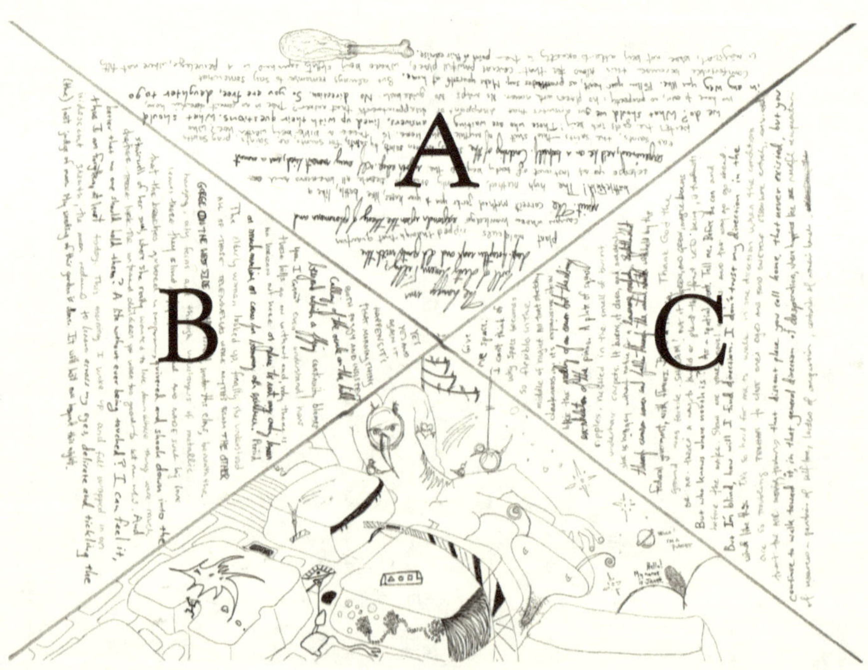

B.

Yes, yes, and again it happens. It's that morning thing, both foggy and insistent calling of the oracle on the hill beyond which a flying continuity blames you. I cannot even understand how these hills go on without end, why there is no horizon out here or place to rest my aching knees or snack machine or corner for bemoaning one's existence. Period. The elderly woman looked up, finally she understood all of those telenovellas were myths from the other gorge on the west side of the island, under the elms, beneath the hanging, oily ferns and through underlayers of metallic leaves there they lived, slept, breathed and made such big love that the branches quivered in response, quivered and shook down into the stairwell of her soul, where she really wanted to live, down where things were much dirtier. There lurk the untamed children you were too good to let run wild. And better that no one should hold them? A life without ever being touched? I can feel it, thus I am forgotten, at least today. This morning I woke up and felt wrapped in an iridescent sheath, the moon reduced to linens across my eyes, delicate and tickling the last judge of man. My weeding of this garden is done. It will last now beyond this night.

C.

Give me space. I can't think of why space becomes so flexible in the middle of the night. All that stretchy darkness in its expansive skin, like the peeling of an onion but the slimy exoskeleton of the piano. A plate of squash ripples, nestled in the smell of burnt underhair carpets. It burns, it does, and suddenly she is hungry without notice for a lonesome melody. Splattershot through crimson leaves and fallen through the artful strait withheld by the federal government, with flowers. It was a flowering. Thank god the ground was fertile. SHAZAM! Out it grew, and grew, magic beans or no, there's a way to build or plant this forest into being, is there not? But who knows where north is? As a spatial event. Tell me. Before the con and before the make. Show me your novel compass and the way to go ahead. But I'm blind, how will I find direction? I don't trust my direction in the wind like this. It's so hard for me to walk in one direction when the conditions are so troubling. Perhaps to close one's eyes and find oneself elsewhere entirely, convinced that the air moving towards that distant place you call home, that never existed, but you continue to walk toward it, in the general direction of desperation, where happiness lies. Needful recuperation of resources: pantries of self love, larders of compassion, centuries of women's hands.

CEREBELLAR ATAXIA

temporarily
closed, with an "out to lunch" sign
on the brain's window

behind a creaking
pulldown of heavy eyelid
lurk the ghost verses:

bloated and out of
order, alexia reigns
as they slip like fish

round the corners of
grey tissue, comprehension's
fingers feeble, slow,

unable to catch
even the last word chosen
to be on the team

pulling salt taffy
phrases from the morass strains,
leaving stalagmite straws

on the cortex floor:
a mess of punctuation
and mixed metaphor

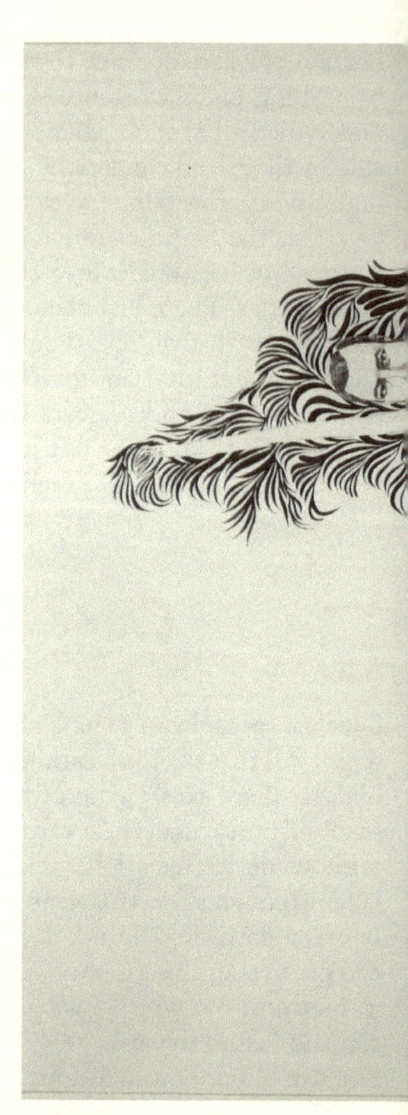

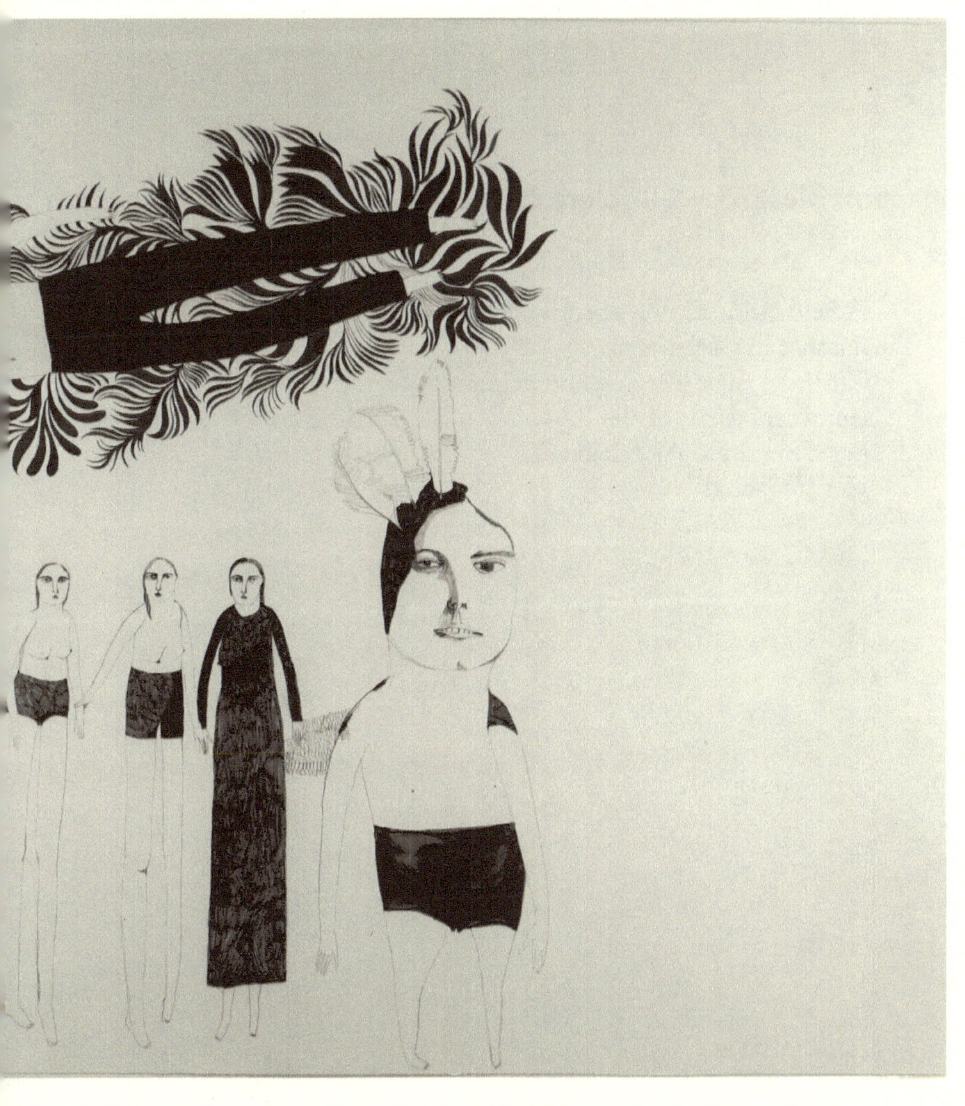

FEATHER HEAD - Kreh Mellick

Chapter titles from 'Obsolete Objects in the Literary Imagination'

i	A field guide to non-absorbable sutures
ii	Ditches in Greenstone
iii	Cutlines: their purpose and maintenance
iv	Representations of the Bluenose in late 20th-century Canadian postage
v	Basic Sundress Alteration
vi	Her ⟦redacted⟧

FOYER

You will wait here forever with the rabbit.
The same one, remember, when the nurse in Germany
told your mother it died,
piercing the needle in much too hard, hissing
"*Have you seen the ruins of the Opera House?*"
That was life starting.
You cannot touch the cupcakes
but like a fairytale,
you may look at the portrait of our leader.
He is well protected
and always shows his warmest features to us
through the black visor of his shiny helmet.
Would you like a cigarette? A last cigarette?
We pride ourselves on replacing the dead bulbs
immediately
and keeping our one plant alive.
You'd have to touch it to know what it's made of.

This Persian carpet is to remind us of other places,
where life once was.
The doors on each side no longer have handles;
they have been slowly erased.
You can go out through the door in the center,
but it's always locked.
If you squint you can almost imagine
that the lights are stars
and you are already blessedly dead.

But when you finally drop, please don't make a mess.
Our floor is polished so that after you fall
you can see exactly who you were
and the reflection of the stars above
that never go out.

The Storyteller

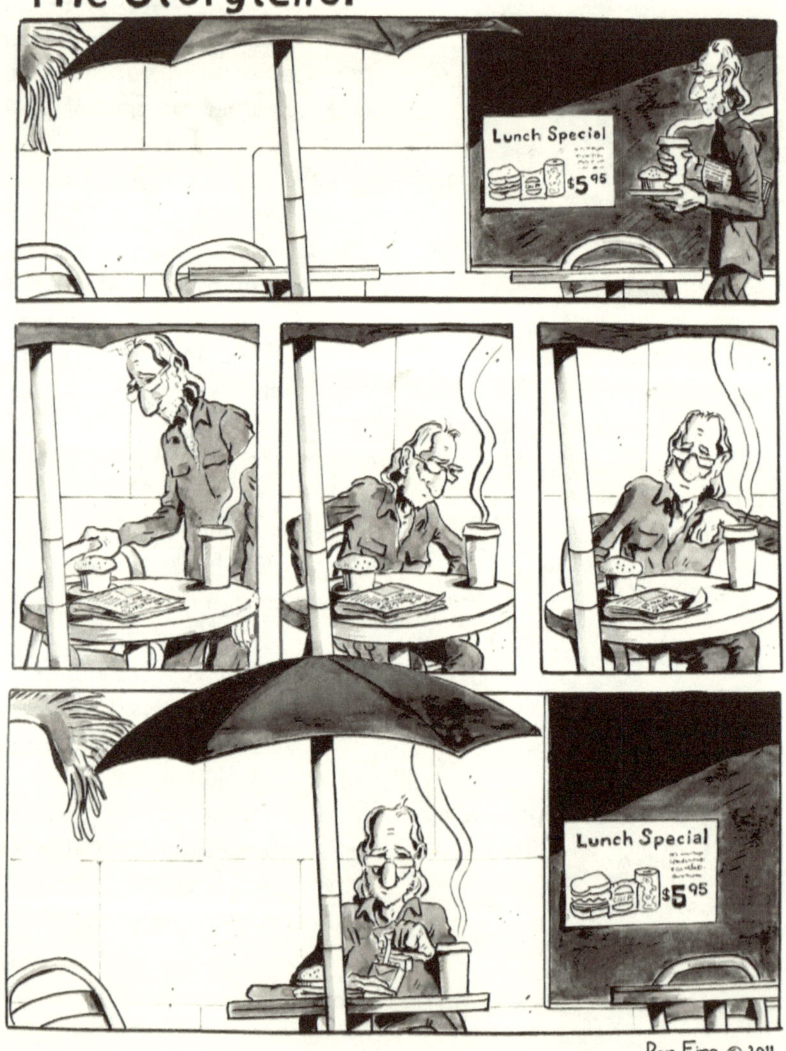

Ben Fine © 2011

November 7, 10:11AM

Two blocks from the half-a-bed I moved here for and now waking up in my driver's seat cot and watching the marathoners go by at mile 9 in Brooklyn thinking about a time when things are different as I eat the last pieces of the Jim Beam flavored beef jerky I bought in Rhode Island last week, even though I found out today it expired on June 28, 2008—my grandmother's 82nd birthday.

Can't help thinking about being in this seat, in love, and driving 508 miles to move to that apartment, not quite two months ago.

November 7, 12:54PM

Raining miserably outside and I have seven hours left until I am invited somewhere, belong somewhere again. Crouching at a shared table in another small library, East Village now, collected a small stack to read.

November 7, 2:39PM

Several homeless or shelter-dwelling people populate the library to capacity. All of us are hidden away from the cold rain. The woman nearest to me burns my nostrils with the ammonia of dry piss-stained pants. Clearly, she can't read. She flipped through one book of pet pictures and now another of contemporary fashion uses for antique lace. I'm not sure she even knows how to look at pictures carefully. Her afternoon is an exercise in flipping pages, no consideration invested in the books or anything on those pages. I just want to read these books without having to be so closely drawn into her life, its poorly hidden darkness.

November 7, 3:52PM

I read a small article on spatial disorientation. I can't stop thinking about the metaphor of it. Pilots in small planes that get lost so badly in bad weather that they no longer know which way is up. Spatial disorientation has the same effect on avalanche victims. They try climbing the wrong way out of the debris and just bury themselves deeper. I am trying to have a real awareness to that issue.

The article said you can dig a little space around your mouth and watch which way your spit falls. Something to discover, soon.

November 7, 5:24PM

In Brooklyn now, I am waiting in the subway station to meet this girl I am staying with tonight, trying to stay warm until then.

I found no church today, no quiet. I feel inundated still. Sitting here while people reach around to open the emergency exit door to enter between the turnstiles. I am unnerved by each alarm, even when I see them coming.

GARDENS

Our brothers dug us graves in the backyard, each one a different size so we knew which belonged to us. We had a fence, and no one could see to concern themselves.

"Where are yours?" we asked.
"We don't need any," they said.
"What if we grow bigger?"
"Then we'll have to trim you down a bit."

We giggled when they tickled us, we laughed at their jokes, we couldn't help ourselves.

Looking at those graves gave half a story, that of the soonly dead. The other half came from the ones destined to last, those stuck behind, left alive: some people are unlucky in living. Call them happy tragedies. Call us sisters, all of us.

Lying on our backs in our graves, joy flooded out from our eyes; we drowned in it we were so thankful.

We had lost our parents even when they were still alive. They disappeared slowly, dragging out our mourning for years.

The timbre of their parentage was rent with affection, measured and wise, and intended for none of us in particular. They offered second-hand attention – passing praise to one of us at random, hoping it would hit its target – and we took it because our vocabulary was too small to refuse. All we knew was to say yes, yes please, please yes, please.

We believed our parents loved us collectively with absent anticipation, the way Alzheimer's patients laugh at jokes before hearing the punchline. We caressed them when they asked and resented explanations when given.

Different lives were possible, but we didn't think to complain. Our brothers said that we knew better than to know better, which was giving us too much credit: we knew when to cut our losses.

Our parents loved each other more than anything else in the whole world. When they died for good, we cried for days we were so happy for them. It didn't matter how they died, and that it didn't matter mattered.

Our brothers were our mothers. They slept between fretting and yelled after us every evening. As a joke they tucked basketballs under their t-shirts and took their time getting up from chairs.

"Here comes another one," they said. "This time it's a boy."

They said this so often we had little time to take offense.

Our brothers were born falling off bicycles, making mistakes before they even tried. With a sandwich in one hand and a letter in the other, they slipped the sandwich down the maildrop every time. They could never fulfill promises, which was something we learned to be thankful for. When they went to strike each other we remained calm, knowing they would miss. Their rare triumphs were the innovative ways they pushed chemicals into their bodies, the small satisfaction of that task done well, hallucinations wrought unto themselves, dreams come true: gasoline, butane, hair spray, turpentine, paint.

We lurched in their waking and squirmed under their fingers mid-morning. Our bed was large yet barely fit us all. We complained little.

This should explain enough.

The story of the girl who thought to kill herself, who found a mix-tape on the roof of a parking garage, who brought the tape home and listened to it, who was talked out of death by music.

She played the tape every morning, every night, during every walk, on every trip, for twenty months. She taught herself to smile. Everyone forgot to worry about her. And when the tape snapped from overuse, so did she.

Her brothers found her head-down on the concrete stoop, Walkman duct-taped to her palm, headphones glued in her ears. A tail of magnetic tape drooled from her mouth, the rest swallowed inside her. That death was a half-surprise that saddened few and was remembered by less.

We wrote that story, each of us, hundreds of times. That story belonged to us, we owned it, it was our story. That should be enough.

We stopped going to school after our parents died. Grieving would distract us from our lessons, we reasoned. Who could be expected to learn cursive while under such duress? And because evading the army of replacement parents occupied much of our time, no one could reach us to prove otherwise.

Friends were the new enemies. We spent our evenings locking the deadbolt, checking the peephole, latching the chain. People came by often, and when they did we pretended we were sick or dying or dead or gone.

The house we lived in smelled like moist shag carpeting, and we scrubbed it without mercy. Sponges shined up the cakey floors. Our wrinkled fingers paled from the soak of bleach water.

The old and moldy furniture smelled like itself, so we moved all of it onto the front lawn, where it looked lovely. And after eating in our new sunlit dining room, we stepped inside to sniff out our work. Nothing had changed. The smell remained, full-fledged and fetid, and it grew stronger as we walked from room to room.

We realized it had to be us, our own bodies, our odor blossoming in the gaps where tables and chairs and sofas once rested. We soaped ourselves for hours and walked around again. We were clean but the air was still nauseous. How else to explain it but to blame our blood? And we were covered in it.

This is justice: levering our bathtub out a second-floor window using rollerblades, a headboard, and two titanium baseball bats. The back claws caught on the sill and wouldn't budge, mounting the tub outside our home like a plane wreck, streetside, full gore, spiteful. We chucked clumps of grass at it for hours each day. A week later the tub was painted in dirt, and we smelled like grass, earth, and sweat: the new us.

What did we do with the new tragedies around us? We buried them.

On the first floor we built forts from the clothes of our parents. Pants became chimneys, nightgowns curtains, six dress shirts buttoned together made a teepee. Had our parents been alive they would never have noticed. Reminiscing about our parents' inattentiveness panged us with shame: all the squandered opportunities, the years spent fortressless.

We vowed to always think of these ideas ahead of time, next time, starting that day or starting the next.

Loudly in our minds, while draping pajamas from ceiling hooks, we repeated our prayer: this is for us, this is for them, everyone stays, everyone ends, swallow the good, swallow again, protect us, amen. Our brothers lolled with addiction upstairs. We hung scarves from the ceiling fan. This is for them.

The top floor was our parents' former bedroom. We put down soft mats and pillows, and played nature sounds from a boombox balanced on the windowsill. Our brothers coined it the Rest Room.

We painted a thin line of grass green on every wall exactly six feet from the floor, with sky blue painted above it and dirt brown below. That, for us, was rest. Lying there in peace, we felt too lucky, like criminals on tropical islands fantasizing about the less they deserved.

We filled sample perfume bottles with lighter fluid and stuck swatches of silk into the necks, then set them on fire and let helium balloons carry them from the roof of our house. When one bottle went off in our hands, we picked glass from our skin for days. But nothing stopped us from going back up later, building more, and watching them explode.

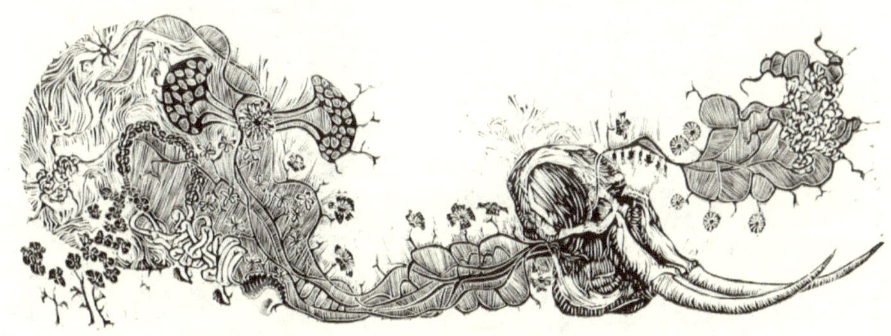

The higher the bottles floated before exploding, the harder we laughed; it hurt so much if they disappeared. Below us, our brothers took poison into their bodies, and this was how we waited to be invited back in poison's place: we laughed ourselves breathless.

Time on the roof was eventful and inaccurate. We careened away from grief like babies rejecting vegetables. We were blissed out of our skulls. Finally beckoned inside by our brothers, we thought, maybe we should stay up here. Maybe we will. Maybe we did.

To Be Continued...

(see page #50 for the exciting conclusion of GARDENS)

The target in question was this reviewer from the New York Times.
He'd come with a photographer in tow ~~outfitted with~~,
notepad, his sidekick armed with a ~~Nikon D25~~ 30-pound
miss in the crowd. Ona was
istached Floydd for the
llo darling" ~~gave~~
ich he made no

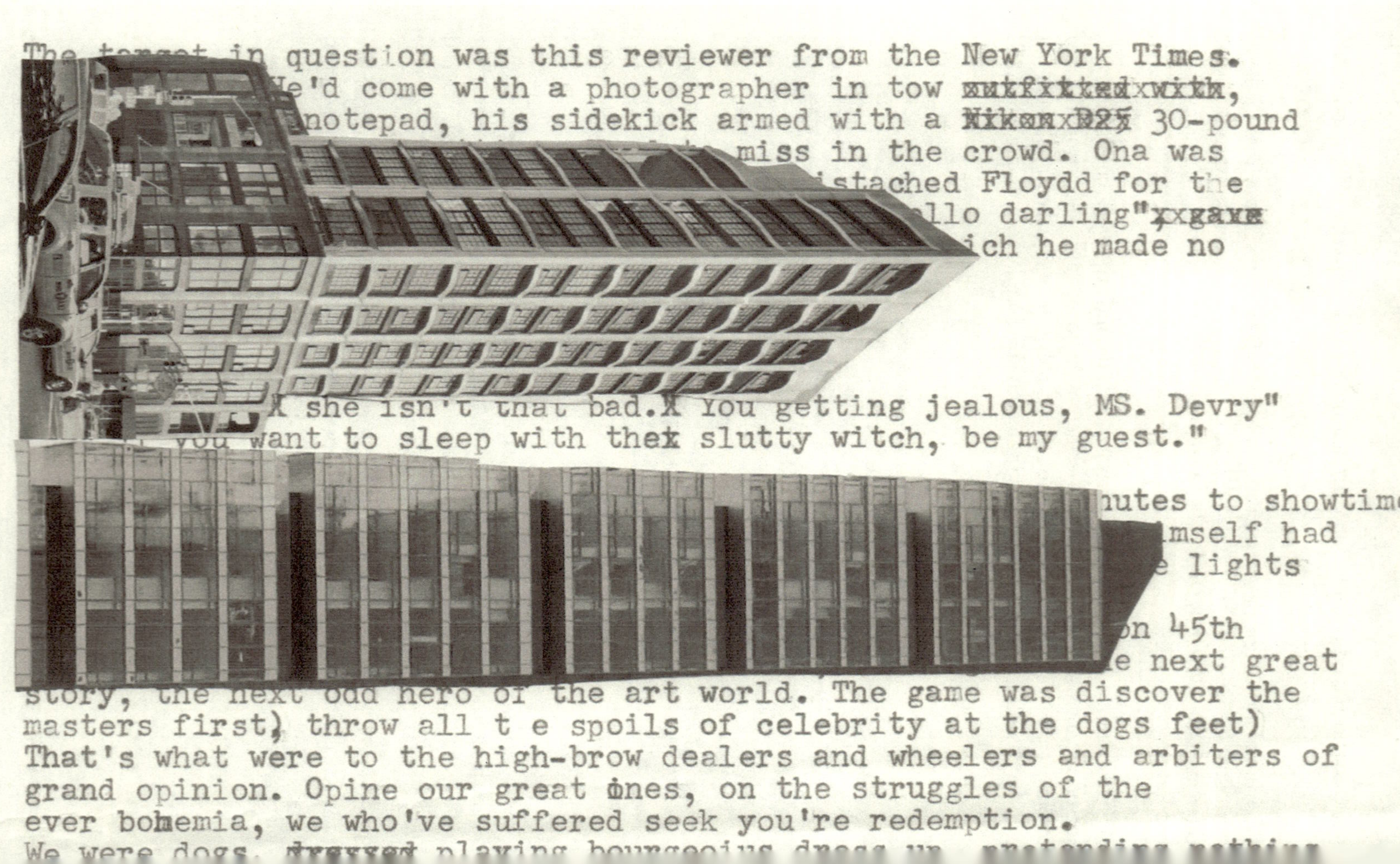

X she isn't that bad. X You getting jealous, MS. Devry"
you want to sleep with thex slutty witch, be my guest."

nutes to showtime,
mself had
e lights

on 45th
e next great
story, the next odd hero of the art world. The game was discover the
masters first) throw all t e spoils of celebrity at the dogs feet)
That's what were to the high-brow dealers and wheelers and arbiters of
grand opinion. Opine our great ones, on the struggles of the
ever bohemia, we who've suffered seek you're redemption.
We were dogs, ~~dressed~~ playing bourgeoius dress up, pretending nothing

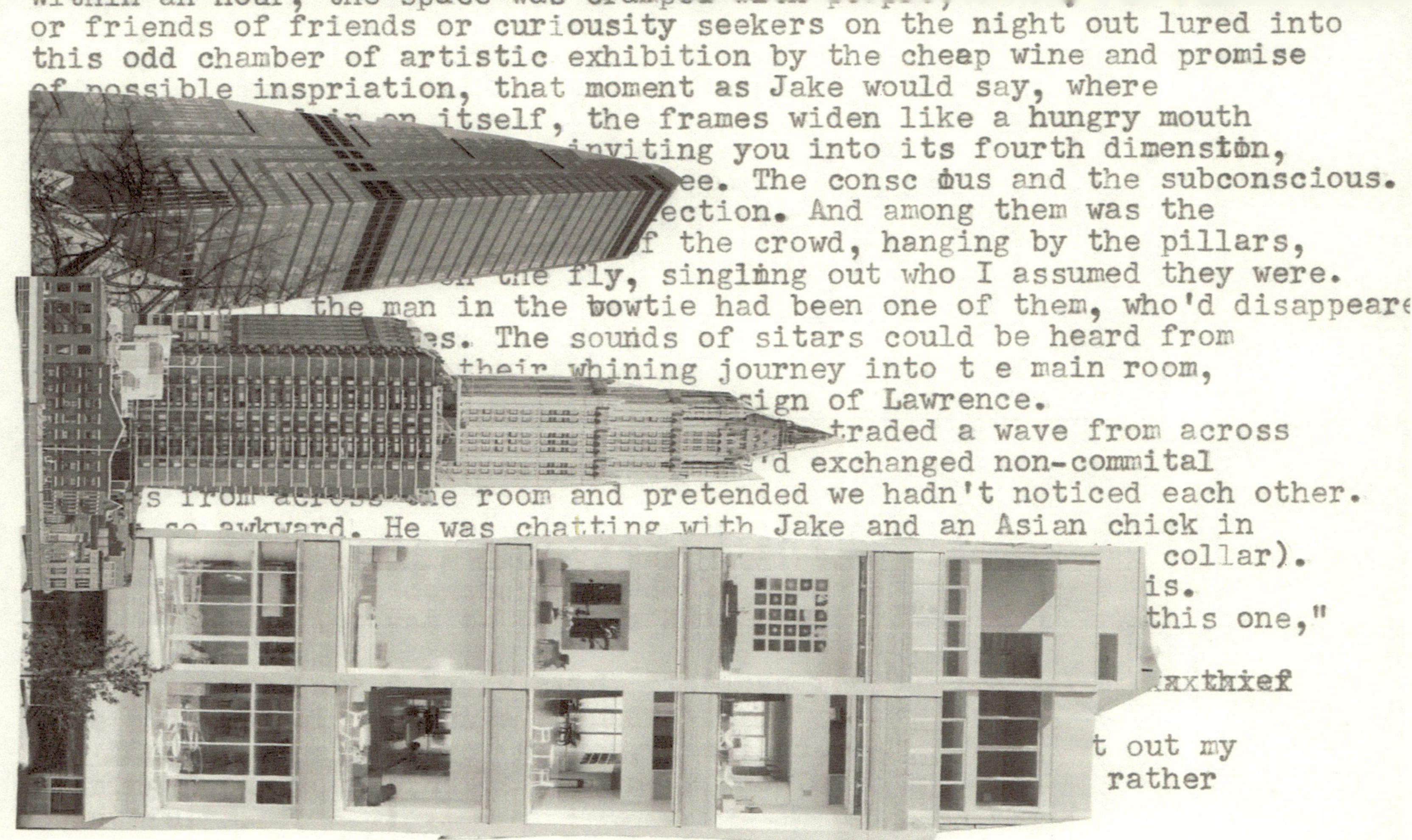
or friends of friends or curiousity seekers on the night out lured into
this odd chamber of artistic exhibition by the cheap wine and promise
of possible inspriation, that moment as Jake would say, where
itself, the frames widen like a hungry mouth
inviting you into its fourth dimension,
ee. The consc ious and the subconscious.
ection. And among them was the
f the crowd, hanging by the pillars,
the fly, singling out who I assumed they were.
the man in the bowtie had been one of them, who'd disappeare
es. The sounds of sitars could be heard from
their whining journey into t e main room,
sign of Lawrence.
traded a wave from across
'd exchanged non-commital
s from across the room and pretended we hadn't noticed each other.
so awkward. He was chatting with Jake and an Asian chick in
collar).
is.
this one,"
xxthixef
t out my
rather

Comb | Prison

1. The comb crosses the room on its plastic mustache.

2. The statues in the cemetery have been given painted-on mustaches.

3. The shrubbery resembles military mustaches.

4. The clouds are old, old mustaches.

5. The new century is waving goodbye to all but the fattest mustaches.

6. With his handsome mustache Geoffrey waxes his new jet planes.

7. The mitochondria is sleeping while its mustache sweeps up the rain.

8. A little girl may someday grow a mustache but never show it.

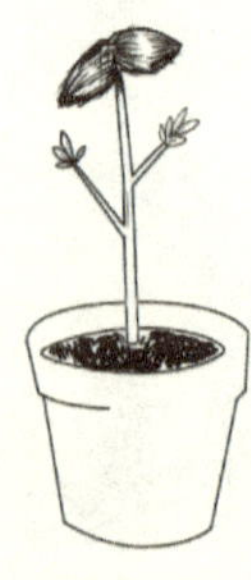

9. While on a date I ordered a rusty mustache from the bartender. My lady friend had a mustache-flavored daiquiri.

10. Today is the anniversary of my old mustache which grows at the edge of my current mustache.

11. I am astonished when people touch my mustache—how rude but also, how exciting!

12. I am able to smell last summer in the curls of my brown mustache.

13. I would like to thank everyone for their letters concerning the health and safety of my mustache.

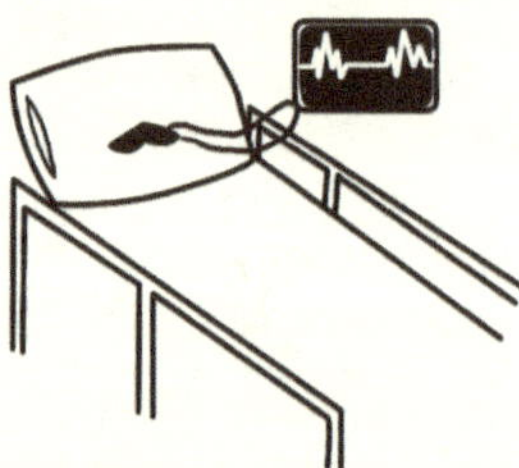

14. In the night it may be the deadly tarantula or my daring mustache you feel on your thigh.

15. I regret this wallpaper textured with orange mustaches.

16. Just as every prison guard has a mustache, every mustache is a prison guard.

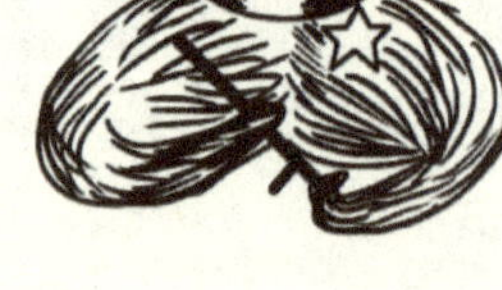

Night | Strangers

17. I talked all night with my shy mustache and in the morning neither of us felt embarrassed.

18. The long garden curves into a green crescent because it has a mustache, too.

19. I can make a mustache out of a small lizard by adding hair.

20. When British gentlemen run their fingers through their mustaches, imagine flying.

21. I am content to let the beer dry in my mustache for an entire Sunday afternoon.

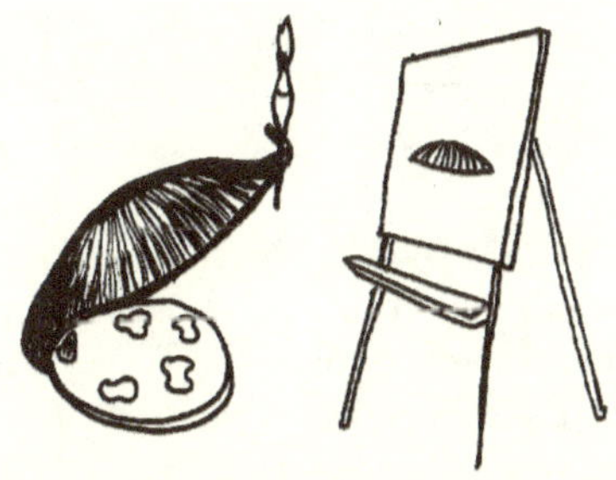

22. I'm in the habit of painting small portraits of my mustache using only my mustache and the mustaches of my friends.

23. I am thinking that a mustache covered bed would be very comfortable.

24. The exact transitional moment when growing meets up with trimming is my most favorite time of the mustache.

25. If you were to chart my mustache's travels and my travels on a chalkboard they would overlap but not coincide.

26. At night my mustache does not need to sleep so it visits with relatives in far exotic countries like Morocco.

27. I cannot recall the sound my mustache makes while I am eating Crème Brûlée but it may be singing.

28. Your nostril hair can grow into rescue ropes descending into the wetlands of your mustache.

29. I grow tired of remembering not to touch the mustaches of strangers.

I DREAMT I WAS SOBER LAST NIGHT

Pack. Pack and get dressed. Only what you desperately need. Just the essentials: a change c clothes, cigarettes so I can breathe, memory of last night so I can stay hungry.

"He's chasing me," I whisper to the leprechaun sitting across the bar. The leprechaun look over, dipping the newspaper just enough to stare my way with his one disinterested eye. "He' chasing me," I repeat, as if I could make him believe me. Still nothing. The leprechaun is wai ing for an apology. I know that. But there's no time. I'm being chased and I have to pacl We're sitting in this bar, sipping drinks and reading the news, as if any of it mattered.

I need to pack. I'm taking my passport, my glasses. I'm taking your touch and this flick of you eyes. A coat. That compliment because maybe one day it will mean something. I stare at th leprechaun's little green body and big eyes through the ink in the thin newspaper. "I'm no apologizing for last night," I say. "Look, yesterday's a different world. I'm not a part of it. understood it yesterday but today the sun came up and my sheets are crumpled and I'r alone."

His mouth moves but the music is too loud. "What did you say?" I ask. And again his word miss me. "What did you say?" His feet dangle like a child on the stool. He hops down and i gone. I'm now shouting at a bar stool, a half empty drink and newspaper sprawled like a bacl alley blanket and I'm alone again in an empty bar. A graveyard of dirty glasses, used napkins and dead ambition. The music still plays as if someone's listening. But it's just me, alone as i yesterday never happened. Because it didn't.

I need to pack. He's chasing me. I need those two books because I can't live without them This spot on my neck because you're the only one who's ever kissed me there. My window sill because no one can touch me there. This sock, because I took it from you when you wen to the bathroom and never told you.

Paper. That dress I wore when you finally admitted: ok, we really need to start using con doms, and I told you: it's ok I'm dead inside. Pens. That moment when you looked at me in the daylight and told me that you would never fall in love with me. More paper.

The recipe for blackened chicken you left at my place, which I kept even after I decided I didn't want to see you anymore. The heart I gave you by accident a year ago, that you slid ir front of me saying, "Here. I don't know if you remember... but you may want this back."

That time on the bridge that was perfect, no matter how much of an asshole you became after The fountain in the park because for just that moment sober love seemed possible, barefoot screaming at strangers. A toothbrush.

That's when the leprechaun came sauntering back in with his short strides and confident posture. He sat down across from me and looked straight in my eye as I tried to fit all my belongings into my skin. The phone call. That time you saved my life.

"Wake up," he said. "Wake up... you don't have to run. Just wake up."

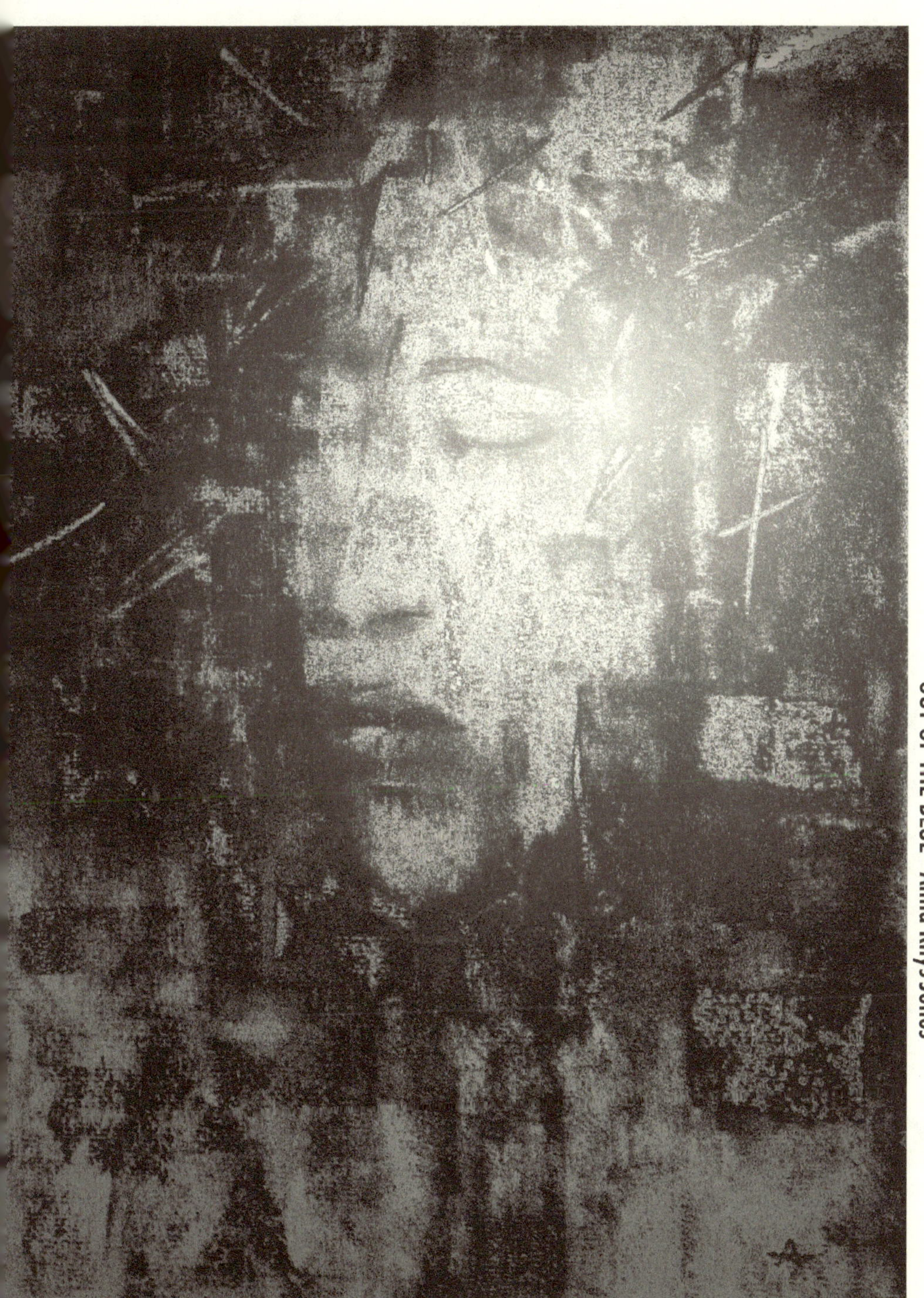

OUT OF THE BLUE - Anna Rhys-Jones

NEWTRIENTS

Twig said,
"ALWAYS GO RIGHT,"
so I do.
so I can prove to the 'hood that fruits and vegetables
don't always win beauty pageants.
in fact—cucumbers kill me,
fruit fucks with my tastebuds
and seeds sicken to dust on my skin.

in subway stations boiling below Delancey,
I wear the same shorts I wore when I was Miss America,
the Kale Queen,
and two sizes smaller
sprouting consciousness of Twig,
as flesh,
supple and starting to dimple,
marred by the singe of a Marlboro Red
that clung to my thigh the night
Clarke and I
drove through Bushwick listening to disco
in his mother's Camaro,
oozes from the leg openings of my cut-off jeans.

"GO RIGHT,"
thighs were celery stalks before plopping
on to her steel sofa,
before the sum of my paycheck was offered
to be her pumpkin patient,
before defeat arose from the beauty contest I had going
with my self.

I've been entered as a contestant against bread:
Twig throws glitz on grains,
praises the talents of the carbohydrates on display at the market.
she's the fudge
on my quest for the crown of BEANS&RICE BEAUTY.

she, is RIGHT.

a year without quinoa always left me in the
RUNNER-UP spot at every personal pageant
I held in the arcane comforts of my
mirrored bedroom.
a year without quinoa was:
lacking lustful support
and genuine Lover's Discourse.

each week Twig shakes
her snappable limbs at me
and exotic kernels dust the thighs—
the gams gushing from denim underneath Delancey street.
quinoa and truth forage my skin to kiss collard green bones
and hug my hips so heartily like I'm a hot potato,
stewing in a wintery crockpot,
when it's the muck and melt of July.
her popcorn kernels explode,
"ALWAYS GO RIGHT,"
so I do.
so the 'hood will toss roses at my sandals
trotting down Bushwick's barbecue sauce freckled pavement—
darling,
how I felt through Clarke's Anglo-squinted eyes,
when Donna Summer was doing her thing on the radio.

Twig wonders at her influence on my
WonderBread ways,
she praises my starchy smile
and that sweet potato sparkle in my eyes—
the scepter is presented to my palms
with dessert three to four times a week,
congratulations, Quinoa Queen,
darling as dough,
and the title is
as the blueberries ripening
in my eye sockets:
both sweet and
tart.

The damn bell again. Morning and I hate my alarm clock. It sits prominently by my bedside and tortures me every morning. I wake. Panic. Even after 10 years it is sometimes overwhelming to face the fact that two dozen 17-year-olds will be staring at me in less than an hour.

Coffee. That changes everything. The future is looking brighter and my plans for the day are beginning to surface. I am giving a first period test today. I take one final look in the mirror and quickly decide that big wooden earrings would work well with my skirt. I slam the front door.

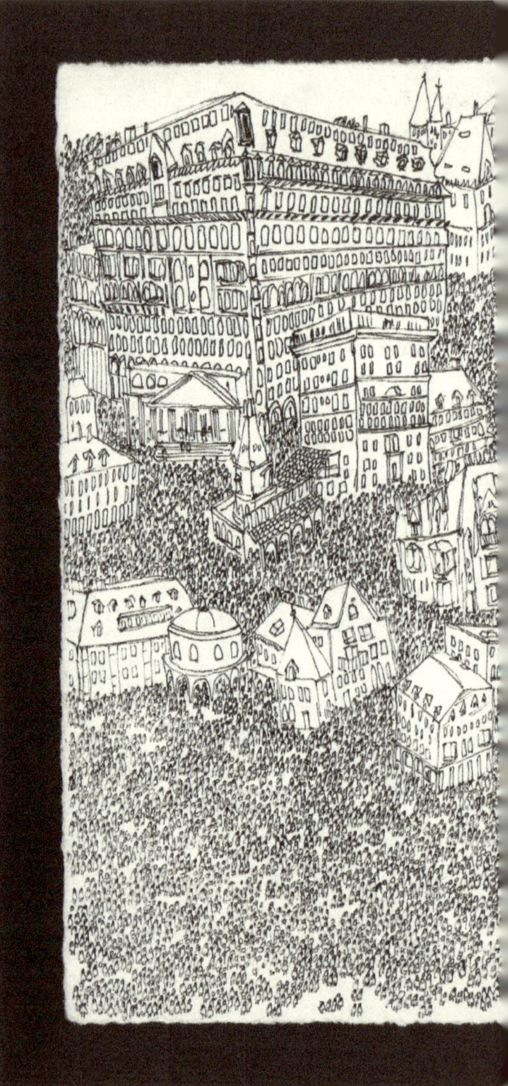

Test days are almost worth the grading. Forty-five minutes of silence. That old-fashioned sound of pencil to paper makes me smile; confirms my belief in teaching; my hope that somehow, something is getting through to somebody.

"Sara, get me a pencil." Tom is ignored. Tom is never prepared and completely inappropriate. Like many of the other boys, his pants fall far below his boxer shorts. It must be uncomfortable. Plodding around with jeans around the hips, balancing boxers and belt, wearing stylish underwear each day. Must be a hell of a lot of work.

Ten minutes have already passed and the class is still not settling down. I feel myself becoming extraordinarily angry. Logically, I know that this is silly. They are kids. My tantrum is not going to make things move any faster. But my 45 minutes of serenity are ticking away. The chance to put all of the discombobulated essays into organized piles; to pour the last of the Poland Spring onto my dying geranium; to compile my growing to-do list; these simple pleasures ticking away.

"Tom, why are you out of your seat?" My frustration springs a leak. "I still don't have a pencil!" The class starts their collective shushing as the clock continues to tick and Tom continues not to sit down. I wave Tom over to my desk and rummage through my drawer, praying I'll find an extra pen. "I have a Sharpie or a Highlighter, take your pick." He chooses the Sharpie and sits. I survey my class with satisfaction. Finally, settled into their thoughts, pencils are scribbling, minds are working, capabilities are being realized. We still have a good 25 minutes when... the fire drill bell rings.

A mass exodus. The act of bustling 2000 teenagers into the wet, slushy, suburban streets of our town. The cliques emerge. Loners sit on the curb. Smoke. Spit. They look generally pissed off at the world. Yeah, I'm with them. Only I can't be. I have to take attendance on the soupy sidewalk. Gradebook in hand, I search for my class through a sea of nose rings and tight jeans. I look old. Not really old, just old-er, older than I feel. I stand out and they find me. "Ms. Allison, no test today now, right?" I consider this for a moment but do not let my dream relinquish. "We will continue when we return to class."

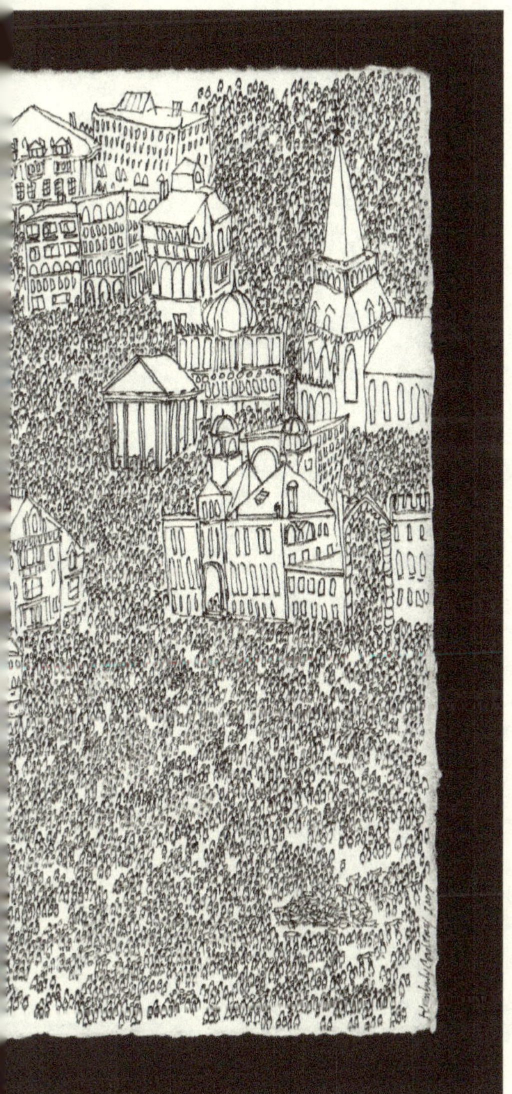

I talk with Sara who is shivering without a coat, forced out into the cold because some asshole called in a bomb scare. I hand her my large, warm scarf. She is new to the school and seems out of place. She is grateful for the ounce of warmth I provide. And we stand there searching for things to say to each other. Small talk between a teacher and a student. One hundred feet outside of the school grounds and our relationship completely changes. We have become random people standing next to each other on the curb. Strangers outside the world of *Macbeth* and *Catcher in the Rye*.

It is over. It feels like the day begins again. The hallways echo with laughter, sniffles and coughing. Trails of wet, brown snow smear the waxed hallway floors. In the ensuing chaos I am able to escape. Bathroom; mailbox; I even squeeze in 25 copies in the empty copy room. Ah... efficiency!

Utter disorder. I enter my classroom to witness pure pandemonium. If I had chandeliers they would be hanging from them. I walk unabashedly into my domain. "Okay folks, the party is over! You have 10 seconds to sit at your desks before I begin to deduct points from your tests." Shock and disbelief; wide, gaping mouths; fists pound on filthy desktops. "No way, we don't have enough time!" "Stop playing, Ms. Allison!" Calmly, I explain that I am not playing.

"The period has been extended and you now have 5 seconds 4, 3, 2... 1. Tom, two points off!" Yes, sometimes the threat must be carried out to gain control. I canvas my subjects. They are ready. Finally... order in the court.

We are reading Thornton Wilder's *Our Town*. I love this play. It was a rediscovery. I had always been reluctant to teach it. I had read it in high school and remembered being bored. I didn't get it. Who cares about Grover's Corners? Why does that stage manager keep interrupting? And why the hell do they mime everything? But I was in a bind. All of the books were out, except stacks for *Our Town*. I studied the fonts and cover illustrations, and eventually chose the edition most pleasing to my eye and touch. I shuffled out of the dry, still space clutching the only paperback copy I could find. And... I cried all evening. How did I miss the beauty of this book? Crumpled Kleenex in hand, I read my favorite line again and again: *Do any human beings ever realize life while they live it?—Every, every minute.*

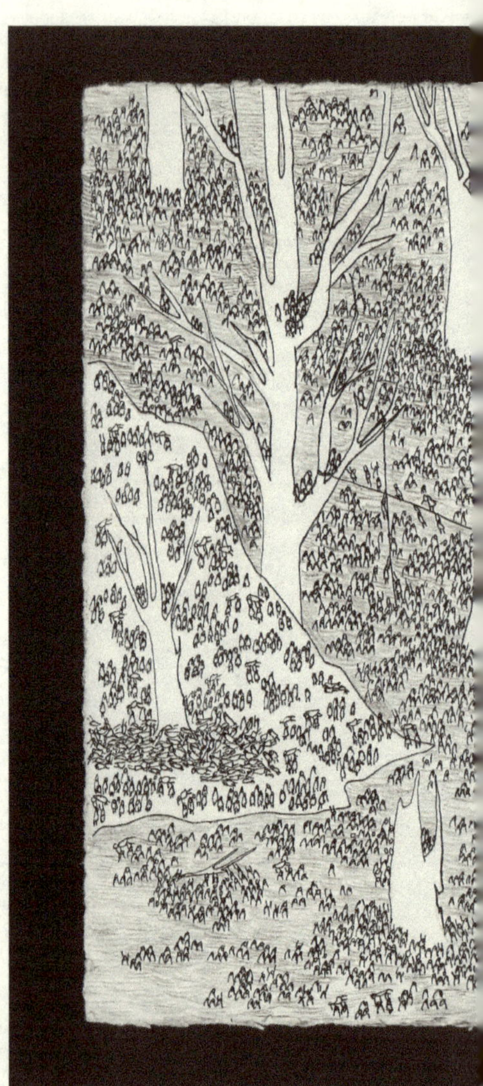

I look at my essays and geranium lost in my thoughts. I notice the clock. The bell is about to ring. No matter how many years go by it's a sound that I will never get used to. Sort of like living life on a timer. "One minute remains before the bell, folks." They are silent now, immersed in the analysis of *Our Town*. They liked it and liked that I like it. And despite their reluctance to take the test, they seem to have a lot to say. They quickly gather their belongings. Sara is the last to leave. "Thanks for the scarf, Ms. Allison, it was really warm." She places it neatly on my filing cabinet, her test on top.

The classroom fills up as quickly as it emptied. I notice Camila. She is always the last student to arrive. She slithers in. Starbucks thermos glued to her mouth. I'm jealous. I would die for a refill. That luxury will have to wait until next period. "Ms. Allison, can I talk to you?" She looks upset. I would love to have a carefree conference with her right now. But I can't. The other students come trampling in and the only thing I have time to talk to her about is that we will have to talk later.

This class is writing monologues. These students are filled with living, experiences too old for the young: a mother dying of AIDS; a father in jail; a brother disfigured in a fire. Camila is at my desk again. I give the rest of the class a few extra minutes to prepare. "I still don't have an idea. I can't speak in front of people. Please I have nothing to say."

I hate these situations. It seems cruel to force someone on the stage against her will. I know that the only reason Camila was encouraged to take drama was because of her interest in music. Damn counselors think it's all the same. Camila is not a top student. She does not participate. She avoids classroom discussion. She will not do her homework. She doesn't like school. Drama is challenging for her. But this is her chosen class, and performance is a major grade. I sit next to her. "You have a great deal to say. We all do. You just haven't found it yet." Reluctantly, she nods. "Let's try the brainstorming activities together again during the conference period." I put my hand on her shoulder. "Somewhere in there is a story to be told."

Conference period comes and goes. It is after school and the piece of lined notebook paper is still blank. I am frustrated and begin to lose my cool. She senses my aggravation. "It's okay, Ms. Allison, this school stuff ain't for me." And the only thing that I can think to say is, "Camila, how about paying attention to detail. Think of the details of your life."

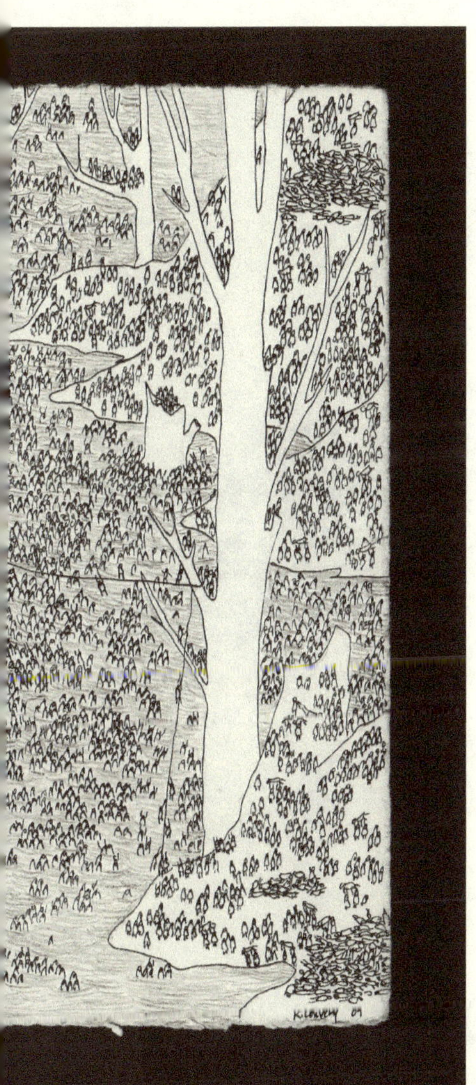

Blank. She stares at me void of expression. And it dawns on me that Camila is not familiar with the word "detail". I try not to be surprised. Time passes. Language evolves. Towns change. Ipods and texting and video games and cellphones. Teaching has a lot to compete with in my town.

I make little of this awkward communication gap and just continue babbling. "Ya know, the little things in life... coffee in the morning or a beautiful sunrise... a new song that you love." Then I take a chance.

I hand Camila my copy of *Our Town*. She looks at me. "Ms. Allison ain't this that boring book about some stage manager or somethin'?" And suddenly all goes quiet in the dusty classroom as I stare at this girl, because for a moment, I see myself. I hand her back the book. "Big extra credit if you read this tonight! Let it inspire you." She flips through. "This is full of your notes? Can I read them?" Quickly I answer. "I want you to read them and add some of your own if you feel like it."

The next morning Camila arrives early. She is smiling. Instead of an Ipod she holds scribbled sheet music. She hands me the book. It is filled with notes. Notes that I am not familiar with. "Extra credit!" She sets up the stage for her performance. I drop my gradebook. Assignments fly everywhere. The class scurries around like squirrels and when all is gathered, Camila begins. She sits alone. Camila, a spotlight and the old classroom piano, and for the next few minutes we are entranced by her melody. Every detail.

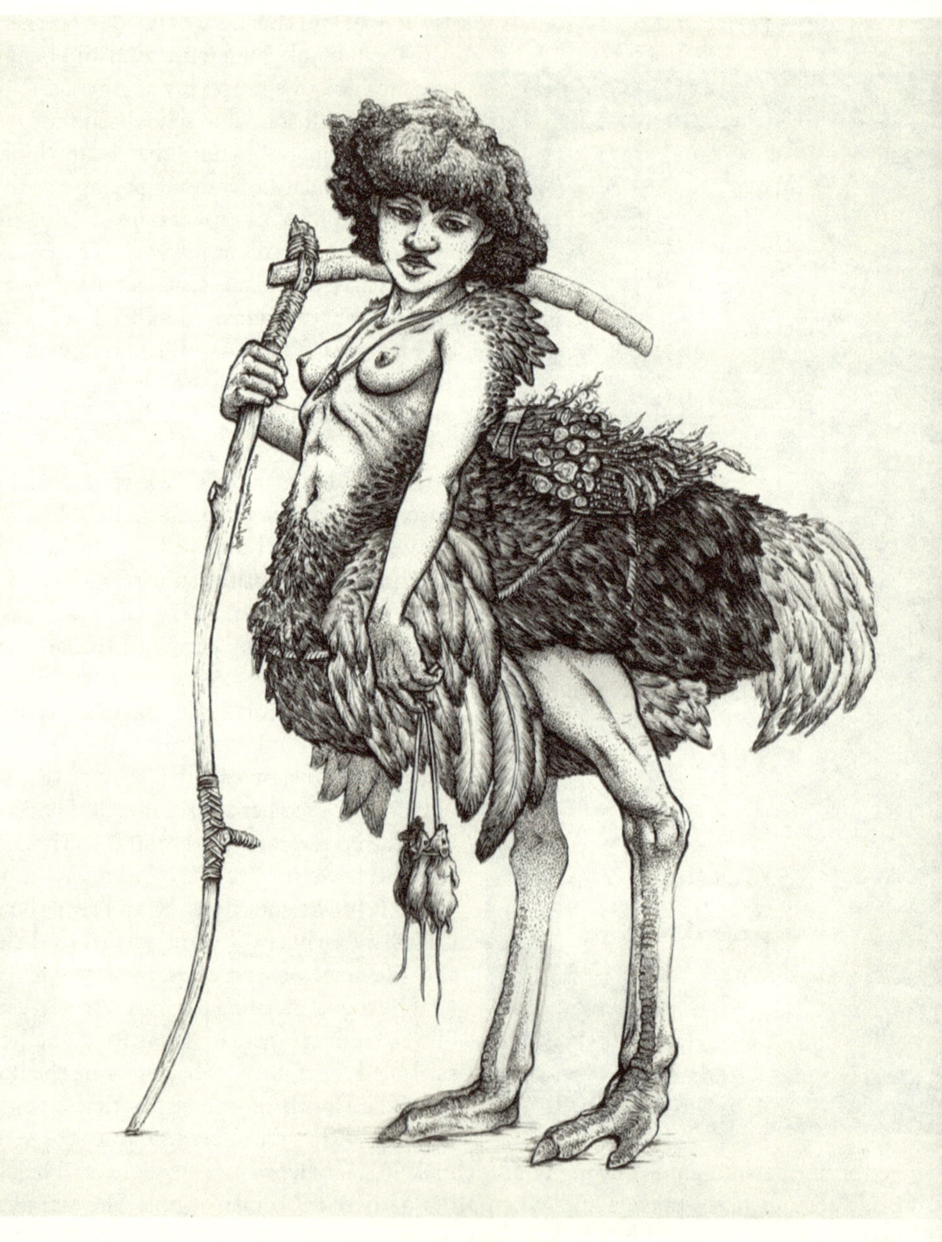

STRUTHIA - Michael Fusco

CAVEMAN'S COMPLAINT

Since I have to hunt
and gather
I would rather
know now
what you
bring to the bedrock
besides your
propensity
to perpetuate
the species

read my lips
or the symbols
I have drawn
on the granite

I really need
us to rub twigs
and create fire
just about
now
or I am
going to
invent the wheel
and roll on
out of here

3. Consciousness is not an overlay.

It is right inside, part of
everywhere and eternity.

The present moment has the
greatest specificity, the most detail,
the greatest clarity. The question
remains whether previous present
moments hold onto their clarity,
defiant against time. Whether each
moment forms a new eternity,
perpendicular to ours.

1. Past moments do maintain their
clarity, within themselves, much
the same way that a distant galaxy
is able to maintain the focus of
every incident inside it,
even though it is very far away.

Every incident, large or small,
is fully developed, everywhere.
That is a rule of nature. Nature
minds the pushing and rubbing
and pulling of everything.

2. The passage of time
is not a fading or an evolution.

It is a perpendicularity of
every moment to the next,
and the sight
we see is the pattern
of a star.

It is a wave,
with a little curl on top
before the break,
rushing across
the ocean.

Many think that death
Death is an accumula-
I realized this when
and I saw that her facts
and archived, without the
For this reason, all of oute
for death, where there is
such a great many fac
deserts,
snow
enough

4. Our love is a wave
rushing across the
surface of the ocean,
two meeting waves
rushing as one.
The surface still behind,
and the surface still in front.
The fronting span before a wave,
speeding through it – as I say,
through us.
The span before a
speeding wave, pulled
in from beneath
the string of the horizon.
The horizon is the
parent of our path.

I once dreamed of a poem, yet unwritten, examining a scene of death...
A mirror hung nearby, and looking therein,
I saw the poem behind me,
scurrying
from the room.

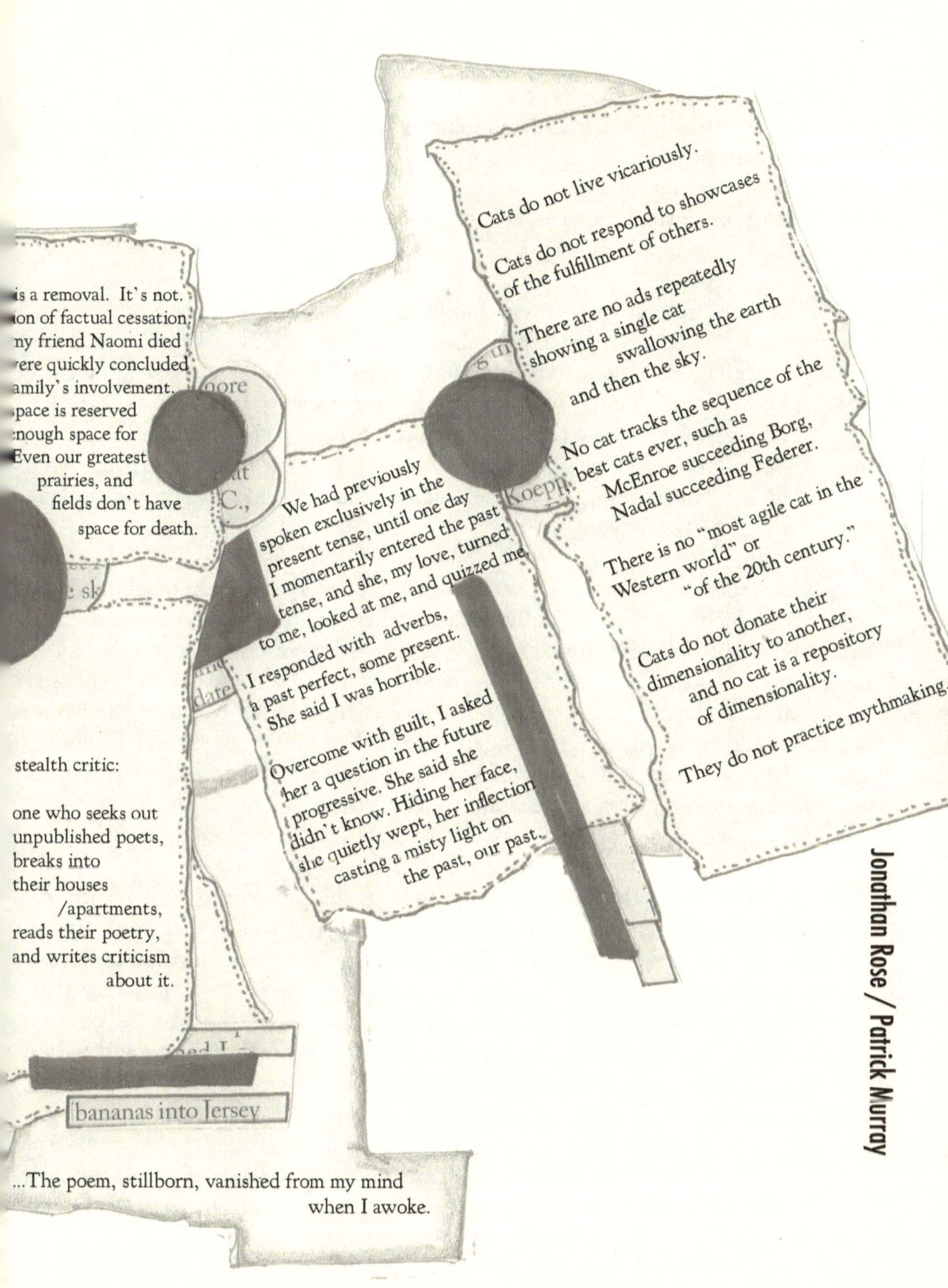

Jonathan Rose / Patrick Murray

THE FRUIT IS SWEET

Winter brings its sting to everything searing the edges with silhouettes of frost and ghost breath as fingers freeze and joints revolt against the bitter breeze under the new rule of Saturn. Each doorway recessed onto a stone foundation brings respite, a hibernating cave for bitten walkers, and one finds himself huddled over the cup steaming into his nostrils, thawing the nerves, awakening two of his glazed eyes to the bright brittle morning.

Inside darkened rooms, caffeinated couples quarrel as she says she understands, knowing that she doesn't but hoping that simply saying will make it so. He has a smile plastered on his face, a struggling smirk as he holds his front—he knows she doesn't know, and wonders if she knows that she doesn't know. For weeks now he has known, yet each time they sit for coffee or drag each other to the new art exhibit around the corner or sip expensive cocktails at a bar neither of them wants to sit at or crawl into the large bed, each taking their own side, he pretends to love her the way she says he does.

In grocery stores, book shops, cafes, restaurants, cubicles, they sleep behind counters and under the weight of fully-packed dollies killing precious hours as they drift from their tasks off to where they wish they were but cannot then be. A complaint, a broken jar, an empty pot remind them (us) where they (we) are, and where they (we) should be instead. But a roof is an expense, warmth is not free, gas is not cheap and though the Baptist lived off of grasshoppers and honey for supper, he never spent a day in Brooklyn. Here there are no grasshoppers to speak of, honey costs more than a roundtrip to Manhattan, and Jordan is miles, years, eons away as we ask strangers if they would prefer paper or plastic...

The catacombs beneath each street are where the rats roam, those with fur scampering about the rails, those without fur hiding in those recessed doorways with gloveless fingers outstretched. The wind doesn't stop underground—on the contrary, it is felt all the more as the underworld roamers curse and swear that, even below the surface, the cold seeps through. Hadn't we thought we'd found an out in this life of running and sweating and hurting and starving and hiding and loving and fucking and rolling and climbing and singing and dancing and dipping our fingers in that magic honey, tasting the sweet nectar and licking the tips, praying (even though most wouldn't admit to Praying) that some Wizard or Spirit or God or Woman would float down from the ethers and paint the world new using our brilliant auras for a palette, the air and our thoughts for a canvas? Yet here we are, deluded perhaps? "We've built pyramids in honor of our escaping," came a voice from beyond, indicting of our careless, self-indulgent excesses and stroking our tossed hair, that ethereal messenger that guides assuring that still-closed lid behind still-closed doors that we are on our way, doing just fine. I say, even if we ARE right, doing just FINE, the cold wind doesn't bow to a ceiling of frozen mud, and waiting for the G train on a Sunday evening below the earth still shakes my bones and purples my hands.

The rise to the land of the living is a reluctant one, no warmer, no brighter, though more active and exciting than the tile hallway, and the two blocks towards my little cubby let me know that it will not be easy, that it has never been easy, that it never will be easy. What is easy? Kraft mac and cheese snapping your fingers forgetting that which you've trekked miles, wasted years, and spent eons to learn, all in a fit of wild impulse and gross selfish drunkenness... But the real men know you've got to bleed to cut your teeth, and that which is hard, the climbing of the steps to the top when you've slept only three hours in the last two days after an impromptu fourteen-hour shift on the frigid birthday of Capricorn without gloves or a penny to your name, knowing you've not enough to keep the lights on or the water boiling or the phone working, with Louise on your tongue but Johanna on your mind...

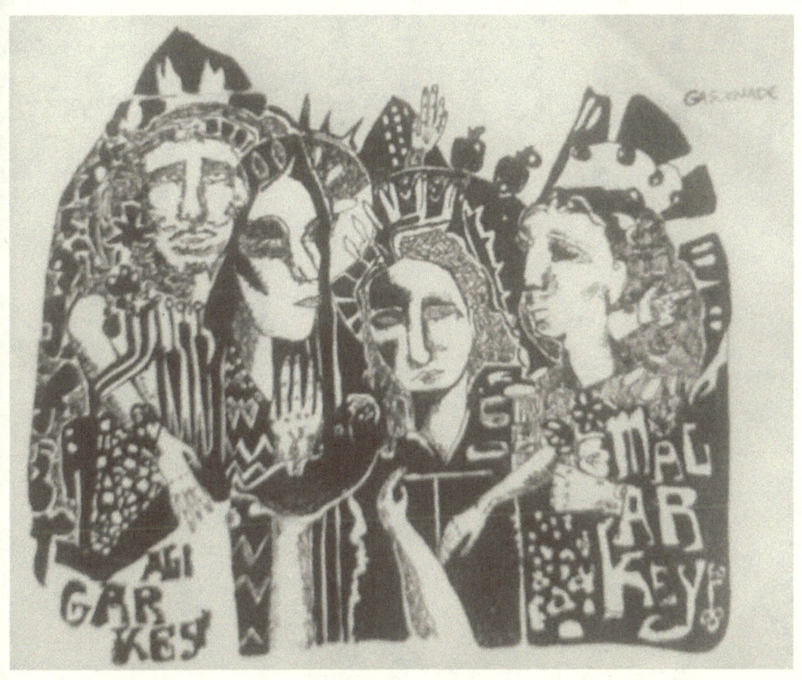

That which is hard, when it's over, warms the chest and spreads like spilled marbles through the limbs, the toes and fingers, up the neck and into the brain, the serpent weaving between vertebrae toward that spot behind blue eyes whispering that the fruit is sweet. And it is.

Fire. Sirens
screaming through
the damning
after-fume, the
gray old woman, towers
hunched over her
battered book, glasses
in hand, she chews them
leaving imprints of her past
in every bite. She sits at the
dark vanity combing fire from her hair. Her confidence
wilts and effloresces in rapid succession. Her plans chew longingly on
her fingernails. Down to dusk. Down to hang. Down to the core burning
quilted configuration that structured her personality.
Everything that is expertly joined is expertly tattered. That is an idea a long time
coming. A walk to the unlearned. A long one. A dangerous one. She might die. Call it the death of a
merchant. Beneath the dark curl of sunrise.

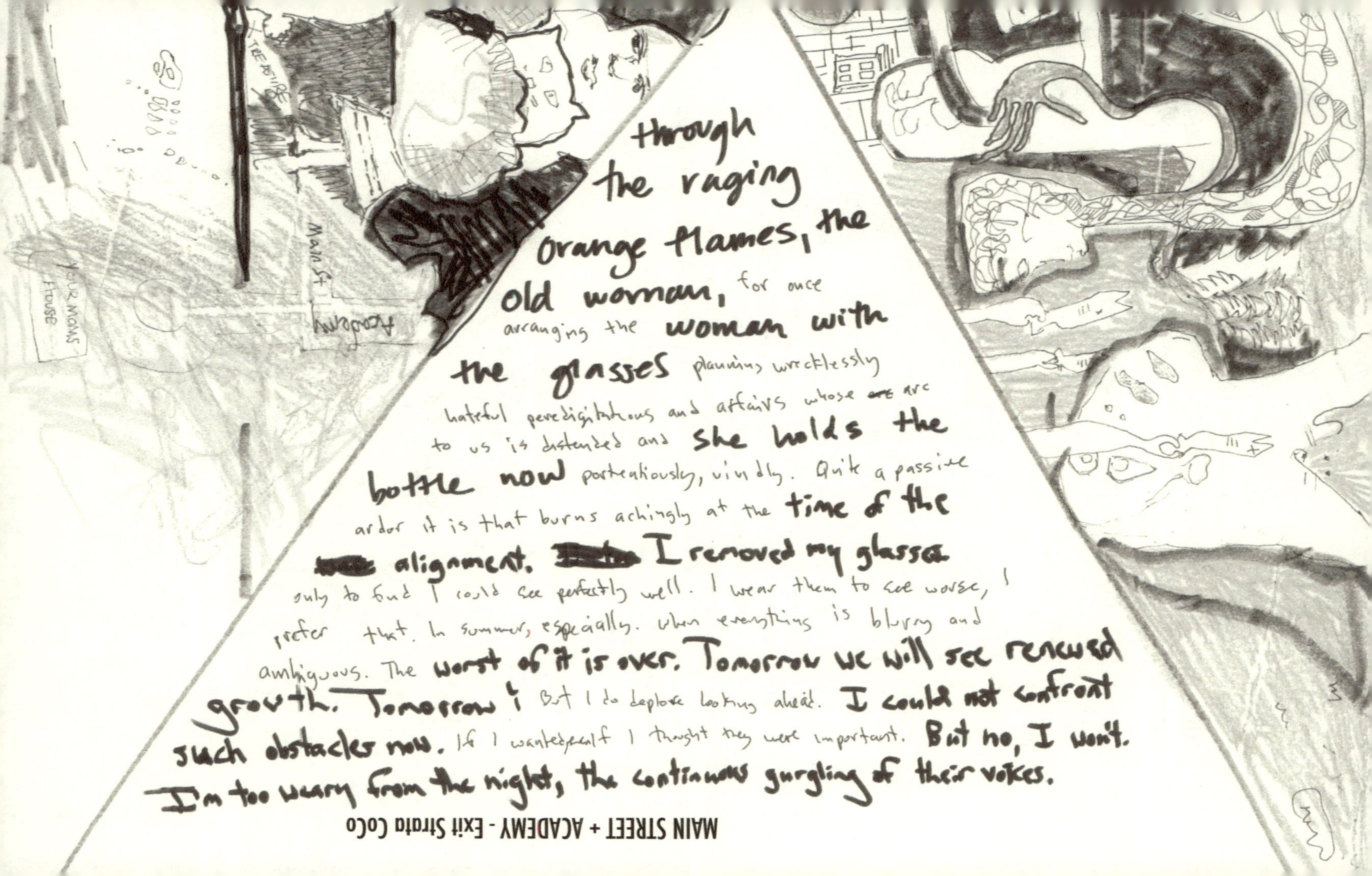

MAIN STREET + ACADEMY - Exit Strata CoCo

A.

Fire. Sirens screaming through the damning after-fume, the grey old woman, towers hunched over her battered book, glasses in hand, she chews them leaving imprints of her past in every bite. She sits at the dark vanity combing fire from her hair. Her confidence wilts and effloresces in rapid succession. Her plans chew longingly on her fingernails. Dawn to dusk. Down to hang. Down to the core burning quilted configuration that structured her personality. Everything that is expertly joined is expertly tattered. That is an idea a long time coming. A walk to the unlearned. A long one. A dangerous one. She might die. Call it the death of a merchant. Beneath the dark curl of sunrise.

B.

Through the raging orange flames the old woman, for once arranging the woman with the glasses planning wrecklessly hateful peregrinations and affairs whose arc to us is distended and she holds the bottle now portentously, vividly. Quite a passive ardor it is that burns achingly at the time of the alignment. I removed my glasses only to find I could see perfectly well. I wear them to see worse, I prefer that. In summer, especially. When everything is blurry and ambiguous. The worst of it is over. Tomorrow we will see renewed growth. Tomorrow I... But I do deplore looking ahead. I could not confront such obstacles now. If I wanted, even if I though they were important. But no, I won't. I'm too weary from the night, the continuous gurgling of their voices.

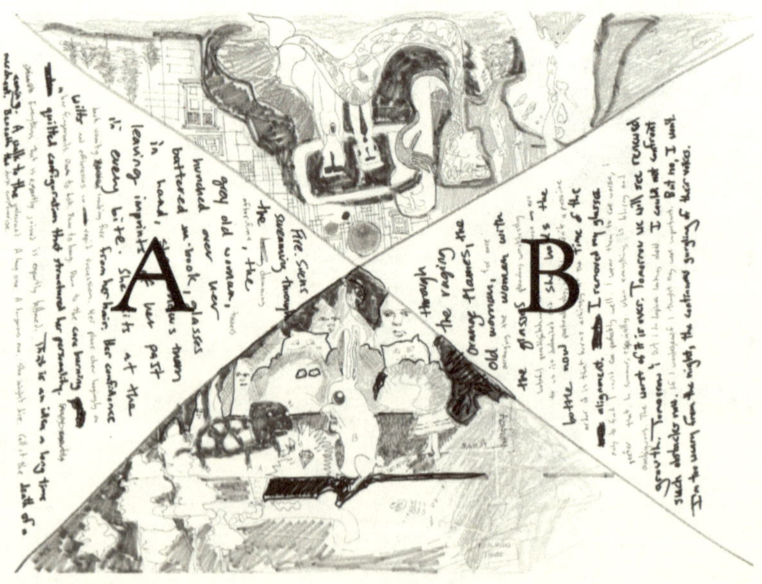

C.

In the middle of a great big city, where the lost porcupine waddled down 5th avenue. A grey clump of pins and needles, the creature seeking sustenance amongst greys and blacks, creature of forest floors meeting starch and linen, gabardine and silk, stocking and trouser. Symphonies of sharpness. What the... and it was a painful tinge tearing my skin, bleeding fluid and putrid, an endless sense of ending. So many needles. All sharp and shiny ready to inject their sense of pain into our arms and legs our fingers and toes. The poor cupine, the concubine of the winter wonderland, she was cold and shivering, her feet dangling, shoeless, in the wind.

D.

Ouch. Dani sat on that couch that old saggy question of a day that went nowhere. Nowhere slow it wasn't even a shimmery slant of a sexy, seemingly sultry singer. Don't ask questions. Needn't know, no need to know. Goodness gracious, sally. Don't you know not to ask questions? Stupid kid. Skirt up to god knows where. Where the hell does she think she's going? Hey can you grab a beer for the frogs? Green friends they just came by to have a drink and put their webbed feet up for the night on a sideboard by the sea as outside the sun glows green like tornadoes coming. There's an ominous sound and I think it is someone whispering my names. It frightens even as it is strangely a comfort to those who seek a certain discomfort, who come here for pleasurable pain.

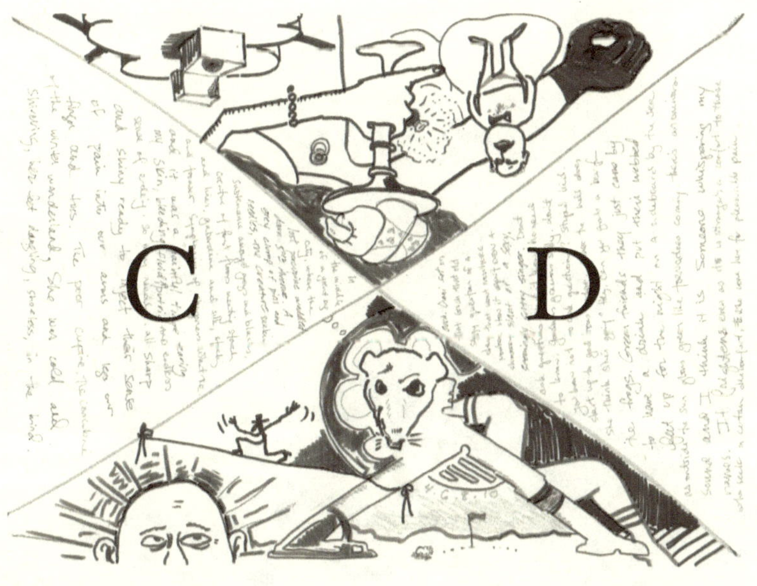

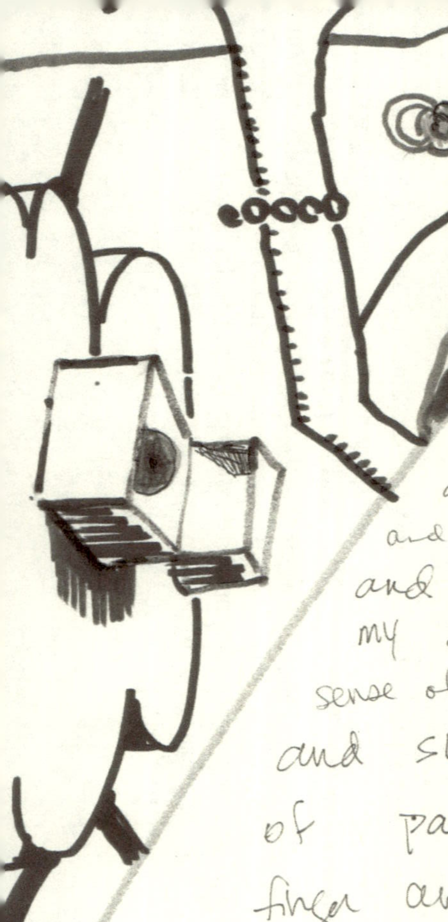

In
the middle
of a great big
city, where the
lost porcupine waddled
dawn 5th Avenue. A
grey clump of pins and
needles, the creature seeking
sustenance amongst greys and blacks,
creature of fast floors meeting starch
and linen, gabardine and silk, stocking
and trouser. Symphonies of sharpness. What the.
and it was a painful tinge tearing
my skin, bleeding fluid, a putrid AND endless
sense of ending. So many needles. all sharp
and shiny ready to inject their sense
of pain into our arms and legs our
finger and toes. The poor cupine, the concubine
of the winter wonderland, She was cold and
shivering, her feet dangling, shoeless,

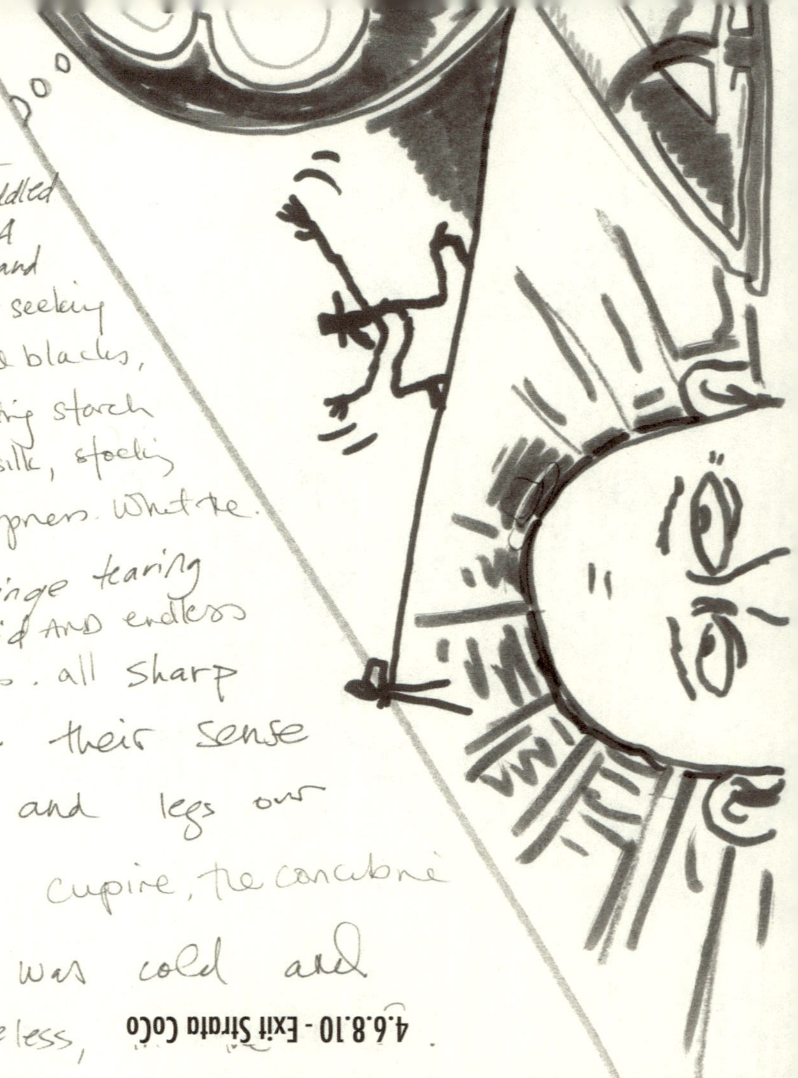

Ouch. Dani sat on that couch that old saggy question of a day that went nowhere nowhere slow it wasn't even a shimmery slant of a sexy, seemingly sultry singer. Don't ask questions. Needn't know, no need to know. Goodness gracious sally. don't you know not to ask questions? Stupid kid. Shut up to god knows where. Where the hell does she think she's going? Hey, can you grab a beer for the frogs. Green friends they just came by to have a drink and put their webbed feet up for the night on a sideboard by the sea as outside the sun glows green like tornadoes coming. There's an ominous sound and I think it is someone whispering my names. It frightens even as it is strangely a comfort to those who seek a certain discomfort. Who come here for pleasurable pain.

GARDENS - *continued from page #25*

If the brothers were hushed, we launched balloons from our roof, and when they fought, we climbed trees and blew bubbles. We knocked out the lenses from our parents' glasses and dipped the frames into bowls of laundry detergent. The liquid dripped down to the ground and turned the grass around the trees neon green, like the trees were glowing, like their roots had halos.

The neighbors saw us, and their daughters joined us. Some nights our neighborhood looked like a fishtank. The bubbles trafficked and collided, there were so many, while our families imploded in unison beneath us. The sound was mythic and horrid, like a chorus of banshees.

Ours was a town underwater, motionless except for the air that bubbled past us. Those bubbles were our voice. We learned to speak by learning to breathe.

A dog sauntered into our yard like a zombie, like he'd come home without reason. We welcomed him with a shower of bubbles. Our brothers screamed a welcome of their own. The dog stared at the back door. When one brother came out, the dog leapt and tore him to the ground. Soap water spilled onto our laps.

When we climbed down we expected to find a corpse; we were wrong, yet we were glad. The dog had one of our brothers by the throat. His jaws trembled in warning, growls rising the closer we got.

"It's not rabid," we told our brother. He gurgled in response. The dog tightened his hold. "A rabid dog would have killed you by now." We thought that sounded true.

We stepped forward with our palms out so the dog would see we were friendly. We stepped closer with our wrists exposed and he knew we were easy. He growled into our brother. Indecision mounted: teeth on the jugular, eyes on the prize.

A popping sound distracted us. We looked up and saw four balloons floating overhead, set adrift from where the other brothers had gone, where they had taken up our tradition. Which one will explode? The anticipation made us giggle.

With a gasp we knew what was coming. One of us saved our brother, the others did not. It's not fair that some become heroes while the rest have to watch their sister torn apart by a stray dog. And it stunned us how our jealousy reversed itself with such grace; we envied that dog, we wanted to take his place.

This should be enough.

We brought our mangled sister to the Rest Room to die, but she didn't, so we fixed her instead. Some wounds needed only one bandage, while others needed a string of twenty or more. The deepest ones we mended with our hands, plugging them up like five-fingered tourniquets. She cried from the pain, and we said not to worry, we'd never let go.

This was our covenant: for every drop of blood she lost, we closed our eyes for two seconds. Our fingers turned red and sticky, our eyelids leaden. Downstairs our brothers moaned in their chemical blitz, and we anchored together like a garden without vegetables, like roots under pavement. We counted the drops, we added the seconds, it was the least we could do.

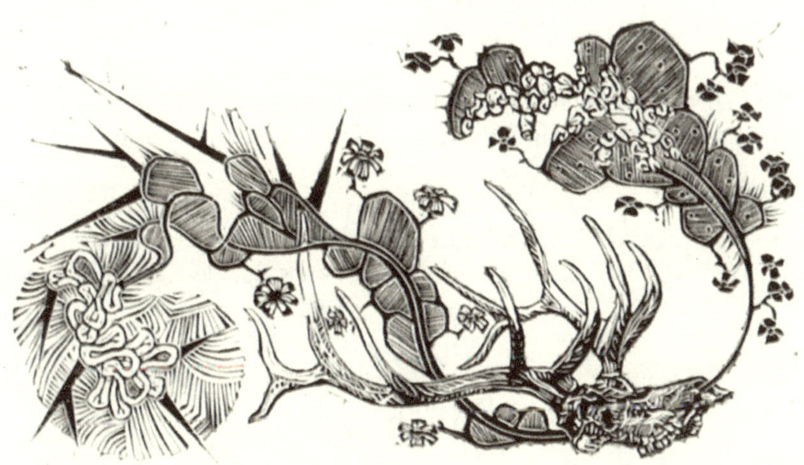

A day has too few hours for such ambition. We were so lucky for sleep.

When we left the room the next afternoon, we stumbled down the stairs bleary-eyed and starving and dangerous.

Our brothers were folded into the graves out back. Their feet stuck straight up like those of dead cartoon cats.

"You can't stay there," we announced. "Those are ours."

Our brothers didn't move. Their eyes were open wide and they couldn't see a thing.

"Come on," we said. "They can't stay there."

We grabbed shovels, we dug deep down.

A group of someones came knocking on our door to make sure we wound up on the right side of a tragedy. "Girls without homes," they said. "It's too sad." Pens flew into their fingers from behind their backs.

"We have homes," we said, motioning to our forts.

"Girls like these end up on the street sleeping in overcoats, sometimes worse. Or dead!" They nodded to each other like choreography, like a crowd wave at a baseball game, like the sensitive triggers of an eager firing squad.

We thanked them for coming, asked for their card, promised to ring the second after disaster struck, and wished them well. They invited themselves inside.

For hours the someones milled about and looked at us in the third person. It felt peaceful to have strangers in the house again, like when we had parents, forever ago, during our lives before death, back when silence hurt less than the words that broke it.

Like our parents, these new strangers glossed over our talent for visibility, and so when we embraced them they didn't notice to stop us.

"Anyone check out the backyard?" they asked each other.

"Let's go," they answered.

A row of upside-down sneakers, set off in pairs, stuck out of the ground and divided the yard in half. Below the sneakers were legs, and below them our brothers. Grass and marigolds and tomato plants polka-dotted the ovular plots.

The strangers stepped off the patio and got on their knees, looking across, content to not get any closer. We sat on the steps behind them, our cheeks heavy in our hands.

"They weren't very tall," we explained, "but our arms are short. We only have three shovels, so we rotated. Our parents used to make us lemonade when it got this hot." We paused so they would take the hint.

Girls in neighboring trees giggled watching us. Domestic disputes whispered from between slats in the fences. Bubbles burst like thunder all around; we leapt up and chased after them with our mouths, letting the soap splash into us.

"What are they?" the strangers asked. They had prostrated themselves, hovering their faces near the ground, as if getting level would help them understand what they saw. A few feet lower and they'd have been right there, and then they'd understand.

"That one in the corner," we replied, "that's a dog. The rest is us."

Graves tell half the story, a garden tells what's left, and always there is more. Everything is not enough.

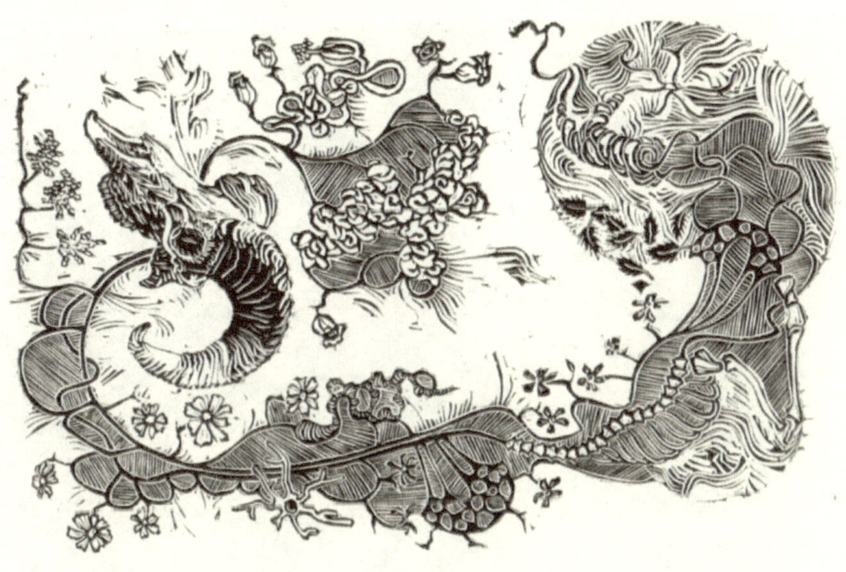

David Meiklejohn

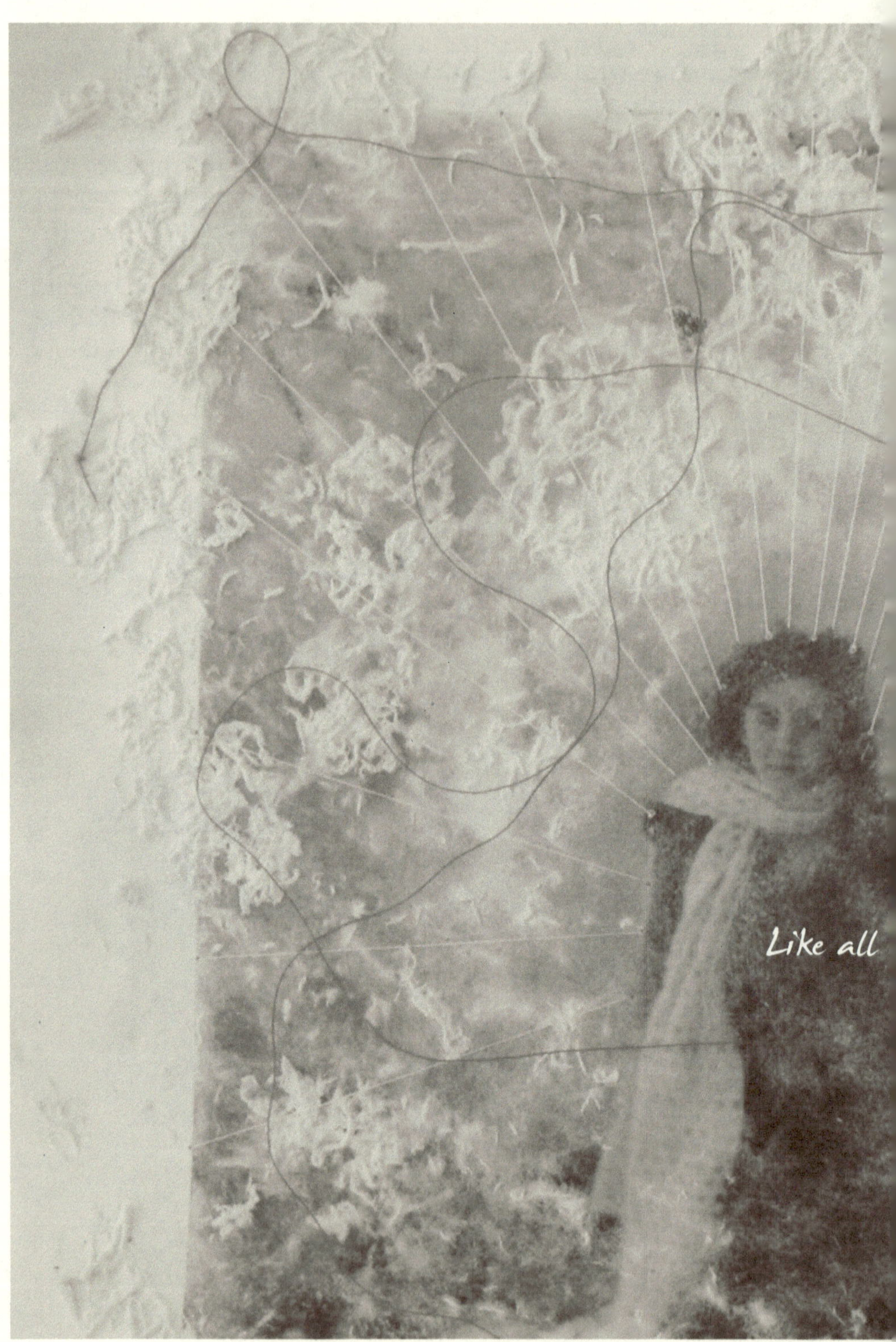
Like all

Interior Plus Itinerary Equals What

All your new technologies, Jonathan
Their trammel and ease, their Sloth Flu and Slate Gate
How they operate according to six basic principles
Web, layer, pipe, fan, strain, merge
Power doesnt count
I cant keep up
All I can do is what you do Pull always
at the disconnected Pinch always the nerve at
the base of my time here
Watch and copycat, Sprint and Spread Eagle
Wait, do you need more of this battened-down Inevitable?
I have a bunch extra
andidates seriously taken I am convivial, chill, and Unlikely
Fat with offerings and oblique forms of begging
Heres a great one:
Dismay and quest, respectively,
guide us

[APPENDIX]

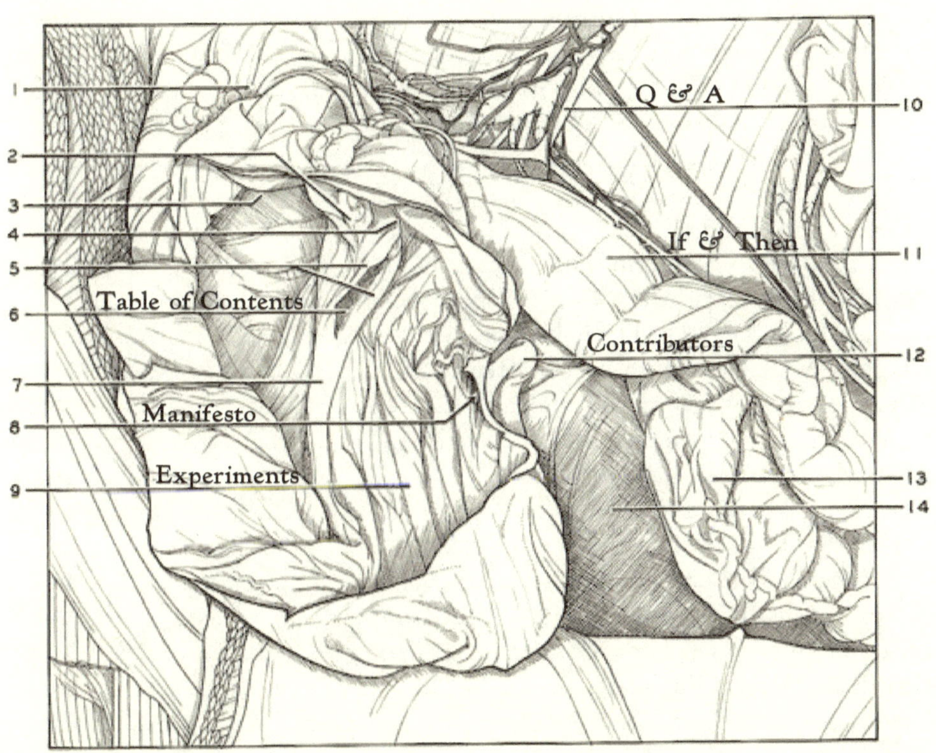
1
2
3
4
5
Table of Contents
6
7
Manifesto
8
Experiments
9
Q & A
10
If & Then
11
Contributors
12
13
14

TABLE of CONTENTS

Entrance & Lobby

Floors & Doors

MANIFESTO

Exit Strata was born out of our desire to produce an art/lit magazine — one that's a Post-Modern take on the traditional literary magazine, presented like a revolving-door gallery on the page. Exit Strata is absurd, necessarily, and is also predicated on harmonious tension: we strive for a 50/50 split between art and literature, often merging the two through collaboration between artists and writers, all playing with the left/right, two-page spread of books (both vertically in the juxtaposition of two pages, and horizontally across the fold) and what can only be done with a book in its hard-copy print form, reinvented between the margins.

But to understand Exit Strata as merely a magazine would hurt its feelings. Exit Strata is a strategy, a process, a community, a creative approach to living life and leaving a trail behind you. Any publications associated with Exit Strata (or its varied eXsT sTraTum) are most accurately described as documentation; of an archive of the production of eXsT that can be replicated in two dimensions. But the sTraTa could never be confined to two dimensions, nor to the timespace limitations of the page; quietly growing in a chrysalis of 0's and 1's, and presented on the inter-web playground (exitstrata.com) which will provide a constant stream of exclusive online content from creators from all disciplines (and those who defy and create new fields), as well as in depth profiles of the creators who make up our global community, across a wide range of disciplines.

The print publication you hold in your hands is envisioned as an artifact, and merely a fraction of our work - which is primarily that of a network of writers, artists, filmmakers, musicians, and other awesome creators. The Exit Strata network is a community of forward thinking, driven individuals and organizations who are changing the creative landscape by their dedication to practice - and to each other. We seek to accelerate the New Way, by creating a place where creativity, too, thrives in and strives for cooperation: leaving behind the Old Way, releasing ourselves from the unhealthy environment of competition and distrust that pervades and poisons our industries.

We are here for mutual appreciation and promotion, with the full and intentional understanding that Network is the new power structure: it is via our Network, and our adjacent, connected Networks already at play on both the virtual/global and local/physical level that we will actualize a new type of life for ourselves, one that places value where we place value. In the world of Exit Strata, creative energy, commitment, and engagement are currency. And you, my friend, are rich beyond measure.

What we're looking for is demonstration of commitment to the work, together - work that challenges, explores, and commits to growth. Work that will inspire us to be better, work harder, and play together. If you are an artist, writer, audio, filmic, or other performer/creator/polymath who feels they would best be suited for our print or web content or otherwise wishes to contact our staff (accolades and financial backing are particularly welcome!) you can do so at editors@exitstrata.com.

ONWARD! We're excited you're here!

- ExSt Exquisite Editorial Corps -

THE Game:

As seen on #12-15 and #44-49, three **THE games** are presented for your viewing (and reading) pleasure. These were created by the Exit Strata CoCo Salon participants in January 2012 at SPACE SPACE in Queens, NY.

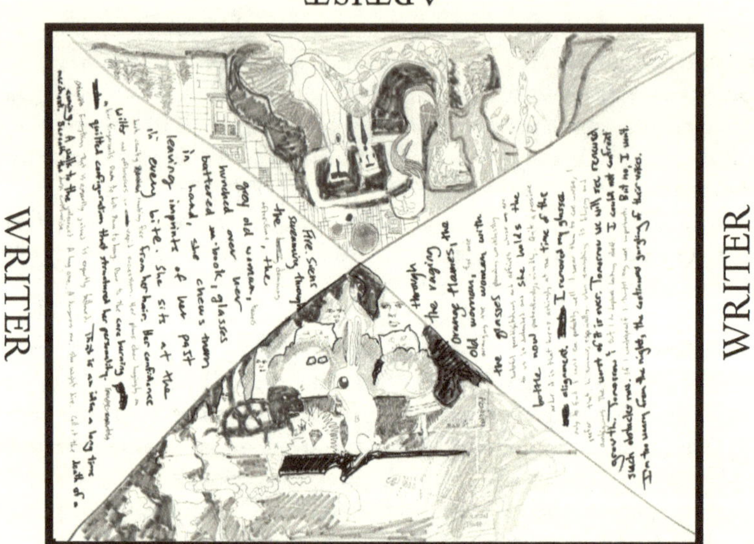

THE, created by D.A. Wright and Stephen Verman, is a spontaneous writing and drawing game in which two writers and two artists sit down at a large sheet of paper divided diagonally with a big X so that there are 4 triangles. Each participant sits down in front of one of these triangles to begin drawing / writing. The game begins with the bang of a gong (if you have one on hand) or by shouting "THE." The participants then start writing / drawing spontaneously (i.e. without thinking, letting the mind glide) until one of the writing participants writes the word "the" (which happens quite frequently in the uninterrupted flow). The participant then shouts "THE" and the entire page is turned 180 degrees so that the opposite writer is writing in the other writer's triangle and the opposite artist is drawing on the other artist's drawing (Ed. Note: varations on THE game involve turning the page only 90 degrees clockwise). There is no pausing to reflect on what's been written or drawn. The writers and artists immediately continue each other's prose or artwork until one of the writers writes "the" again and the page turns another 180 degrees. Repeat until the triangles are complete.

EXPERIMENTS & GAMES

Surrealist Games:

Most people are familiar with the drawing version of the surrealist game known as the **Exquisite Corpse,** invented by French poet and founder of Surrealism André Breton. In the game, one artist draws the head of a figure, folds the paper and hands it over to another artist who draws the body (with the head unseen), folds again, and then the legs/feet are drawn by a third (with the rest of the body unseen). Unfold the paper and voila, a weird little creature inspired by the collective inspiration of three minds.

Sadly the original writing version of the Exquisite Corpse is rarely played anymore. It follows the same model of folding the paper and keeping the previous creation hidden, but purely with words. The first participant writes an adjective and noun, then folds and hands over the paper to another who writes a verb and passes it to the last participant who writes another adjective and noun. Here's an example from our CoCo salon:

"My bevelled mallard
escapes
the ancient ire"

The Exquisite Corpse was just one of many games the Surrealist writers played in order to develop methods of "automatic writing" and explore that liminal space between the conscious and unconscious mind through the "pure psychic automatism" of creation without intention. Arguably more engaging than the Exquisite Corpse are two lesser-known writing games: **Questions & Answers** and **If & Then**. In Questions & Answers, one participant writes a question on a piece of paper, which is folded over, and then the other participant writes a blind response. In If & Then, a participant writes an "if" clause on a piece of paper, which is folded over, and then the other participant writes a "then" clause.

The following pages are the Questions & Answers and If & Thens from our first Exit Strata CoCo Salon.

QUESTIONS & ANSWERS

Q; Where are the rare barking deer?
A: The clouds are a mysterious blue.

Q: What is better than love?
A: Tomorrow hopefully, but you can't wait on weather.

Q: What is the shape of a turnip to the believer of the flame?
A: They're only pigeons, sweetheart.

Q: If you answer the telephone, what will you remember?
A: Leave the semantics for symmetry.

Q: Will I always be this tall?
A: It was running—but I'm better now.

Q: How do I count all the feathers on a dove before my love dies?
A: I always thought it smelled more like apple blossoms—all Richmond.

Q: Why is it called pudding?
A: When the bird does not wake up in your hand.

Q: Why do my boobs hurt?
A: I believe it means a type of leaf, how they grow off alternating sides of the twig—two per node.

Q: Why are you alive?
A: When the clouds thin out to the thickness of lost souls.

Q: Do you think Santa will remember me this year?
A: You will know it when your heart hits its final beat.

Q: Will the ocean fill with rubbish?
A: Add blood. It will lend its unique color.

Q: Is revolution the only way?
A: Sometimes, I think she will.

Q: Why do I love the smell of gasoline?
A: I don't know. Who cares?

Q: Slowly the dead will return...
A: Never! Not now, not ever. Or, well... let's make that 'maybe'. A definite maybe.

Q: How do you say 'I love you' in Sanskrit?
A: Walk to the end of the street, find the man in the green raincoat, he will have a box. Take the box to the woman two blocks down in the cigar shop then ask, again. She will know the answer.

QUESTIONS & ANSWERS

Q: Do animals have souls?
A: Because there is no other option.

Q: Why do I crave for bitter?
A: In the center of the city you will find her.

Q: How can a world be so full of strangers?
A: Ask again in ten minutes.

Q: Where is this train headed?
A: Because I fell in love with your mother. That's right. Your mother.

Q: Why are they yelling at me?
A: Just too tired.

Q: How do you measure the height of the sky?
A: Every second tuesday.

Q: How does one get half a stubborn cork out of a tight bottle neck?
A: Disco.

Q: Who can construe this for me?
A: There is only one.

Q: Why didn't I wear pants in the supermarket?
A: No, i'm sure it's not mine.

Q: Will sticks and stones really...?
A: I'm glad you asked. Purpose, drive, and a delicate disposition.

Q: Why haven't we slept together yet?
A: Rigor mortis.

Q: When does time end?
A: The african dance of the gazelle.

Q: How will we lift this?
A: Two cups of salt, and the blood of future children.

Q: What becomes of the blind man's parrot?
A: Quite far away, but be not daunted.

Q: What is the meaning of this, sonny?
A: Take the number of bubbles in your spit, divide by how many good lays you've had in the last 2.5 lunar cycles, and subtract any lost digits.

QUESTIONS & ANSWERS

Q: Can I give you my number, snowflake?
A: Lovers torn and satisfied.

Q: Why does it feel so bad?
A: Getting as far away as quickly as possible will help.

Q: Where are my green flannel pajamas?
A: The long rains of summer in cambodia.

Q: When do you despair?
A: Intercourse.

Q: You have been on the bus with the cracked glass for years—when does the trip end?
A: A quill + ink

Q: Where can I purchase the finest tuna sandwich?
A: Walt Disney presents: the robin hood.

Q: Where'd all that sexiness go in life?
A: Light years and light years away.

Q: If I bring the cake, will you bring the salad?
A: Analogue smanalogue.

Q: Why does the snow turn such an ugly color?
A: A paper jam.

Q: How many monkeys fit in a barrel?
A: Tar and feather

Q: How did that happen again?
A: The systematic betrayal of the fashion industry.

Q: What are little girl-boys made of?
A: Bigger than you can imagine.

Q: Why does the sun rise in the east?
A: One enormous circle.

Q: Why can't you open your heart?
A: Harder, honestly.

Q: If I stuff a red fox, will it still be able to hunt me?
A: Murder in the sunshine.

Q: Can robots feel?
A: When you jump off the bridge into the icy water, you fool.

IF & THENS

If the world were to end tomorrow, then I could see your soul.

If each morning felt like flying, then other, more arcane modes of conscription must be employed.

If you were mine, would I be gay?

If the world ends tomorrow, the maps might be forgeries after all.

If I drink all the coffee in Brooklyn, then I would smile.

If beauty was an object, then I would hold you and kiss you.

If I leapt from a ten-story building with a cape, then, only then, can we dance.

If we all push together, then God would appear, finally.

If it grows and grows and grows, then Mercury would escape its orbit.

If I knew how to swim, then you might risk losing the fraudulent offering.

If the detectives fail, all of her cells might explode.

If I had some money, then it's all downhill from there.

If it's not under the larches, everything ends. Blackness.

If shadows are betrayals, I would show you my heart.

If the exchange is sappy and flawed....

If only I knew how to fix this toaster, then I can finally be happy.

If I could be anything, then I would certainly find solace.

If I didn't love you, then I would marry you this minute.

If you really think about it, then the very streets will begin to shine.

If candy was my name, paper would walk away.

Ada Athorp, the daughter of a Band-Aid and a lumberjack, is Libra Canibra – a Maine stone soup bil'dah, friend of Blue Babe and the pancake stack.

Anna Rhys-Jones is an artist and teacher based in the English West Country.

Andrew Breitenberg is a street artist based in Cape Town, South Africa and writes under the Hebrew name Selah, which means "pause and reflect on what you've seen and heard."

Kimberly Convery survives by the sea enticing the inhabitants of the village with moments of wonder, absurdity, and microcosmic drawings eluding to past and future that is the now.

Carl Ferrero is an artist who lives and works in Brooklyn and his favorite flavor is Neapolitan.

Benjamin Fine, artist and tough guy currently living in the Bronx, NY, was born with a double hernia on the 3rd floor of the Long Island Jewish Hospital.

Michael Fusco is a California-raised, Brooklyn-based artist who spends his days meticulously pouring over a never-ending stream of sketchbooks and journals.

Paul Gittleman is a writer and an illustrator who lives with his wife in his own mind but may get priced out due to gentrification.

Kevin William Reed is an artist from Monroe, CT (and a self-proclaimed creep who wishes he had more time to bake).

Kreh Mellick lives in Asheville, NC, and thinks that lederhosen are charming.

John McLane was born in a bathtub in a 5th Avenue penthouse, paints with shotguns, and loves classical music.

Patrick Murray is from the materials science lab, and he wonders when they'll notice he's gone missing again.

CONTRIBUTORS · ART

Garrett Deming is a musician currently living in Brooklyn, NY where he hunts rats with low-caliber rifles and dances to Motown music in the aisles of grocery stores.

Peter Milne Greiner grew up on a defunct wildlife sanctuary in Massachusetts and is an amateur astronomer.

Ivan Jenson is a poet and novelist from East Village, who finds inspiration in non-pharmaceutically induced hallucinations both sensual, savage, and panoramically paranoid.

Stacey Lawrence is a poetry and drama teacher from South Orange, NJ, who enjoys avoiding unnecessary disclosure to foster a sense of mystery.

Max Leach works with digital media and lives in Brooklyn with his wife and new daughter.

David Meiklejohn is a pink-obsessed writer and filmmaker from Portland, Maine, and he agrees with you.

Bethany O'Grady is a writer from Brooklyn, NY.

Frank Ortega is a Trip Leader through Chaos and Time, resides in Cold Spring, NY and cannot stop foretelling the future.

Sarah Pinder lives in Toronto, ON, with three large mason jars of buttons.

Penny Pollak is a storyteller who was found on a street corner on Euclid Avenue outside of a 99 cents store and spends her time sweeping up in the apothecary.

Tobias Sturt lives in East London, UK and wears too many hats, although at least not all at once.

EDITORS

D.A. Wright is a fictionist who should not be trusted with industrial machinery. He spends long hours in the dark thinking about the collective unconscious and is prone to tirades on the great accident of humanity. He is the author of Arbitrary Nonsense and is currently working on his second novel The Last Days of Lawrence X. Polk.

Lynne DeSilva-Johnson prefers to be described in the universal language we've only begun to (re-)learn. In lay English she can be called Poet, Educator, Philosopher, Alchemist, Friend, Artist, Writer, Healer, Conduit, Rogue, Free Spirit, Instigator and occasionally Curmudgeon. Her students think she is Eccentric, and she likes that very much indeed. She can be found at The Trouble with Bartleby, via @onlywhatican, and lurking in the cobwebbed corners of the mental universe.

Benjamin Wiessner appreciates a well placed em dash. He still listens to that song by Petey Pablo and he believes in the untapped culinary power of country ham. He values sensible footwear. He always keeps a tent in his trunk. He was raised to witness the emancipatory power of storytelling. These are all source texts for his aesthetics.

Jonathan Rose tries to make words sound good together, wonders what is the most complex thing, enjoys days of intrepid travel, and tries not to stare at the Sun too much. He is currently at work on eight short stories. Bats lefty.

Exit Strata: Print!
Volume No. 1

Type Fonts: Myriad Pro, LTC Kennerley, Futura
Printer: Lightning Source, La Vergne, TN

Exit Strata is published twice annually
Submissions accepted year-round

Please explore our creative community online at:
www.exitstrata.com

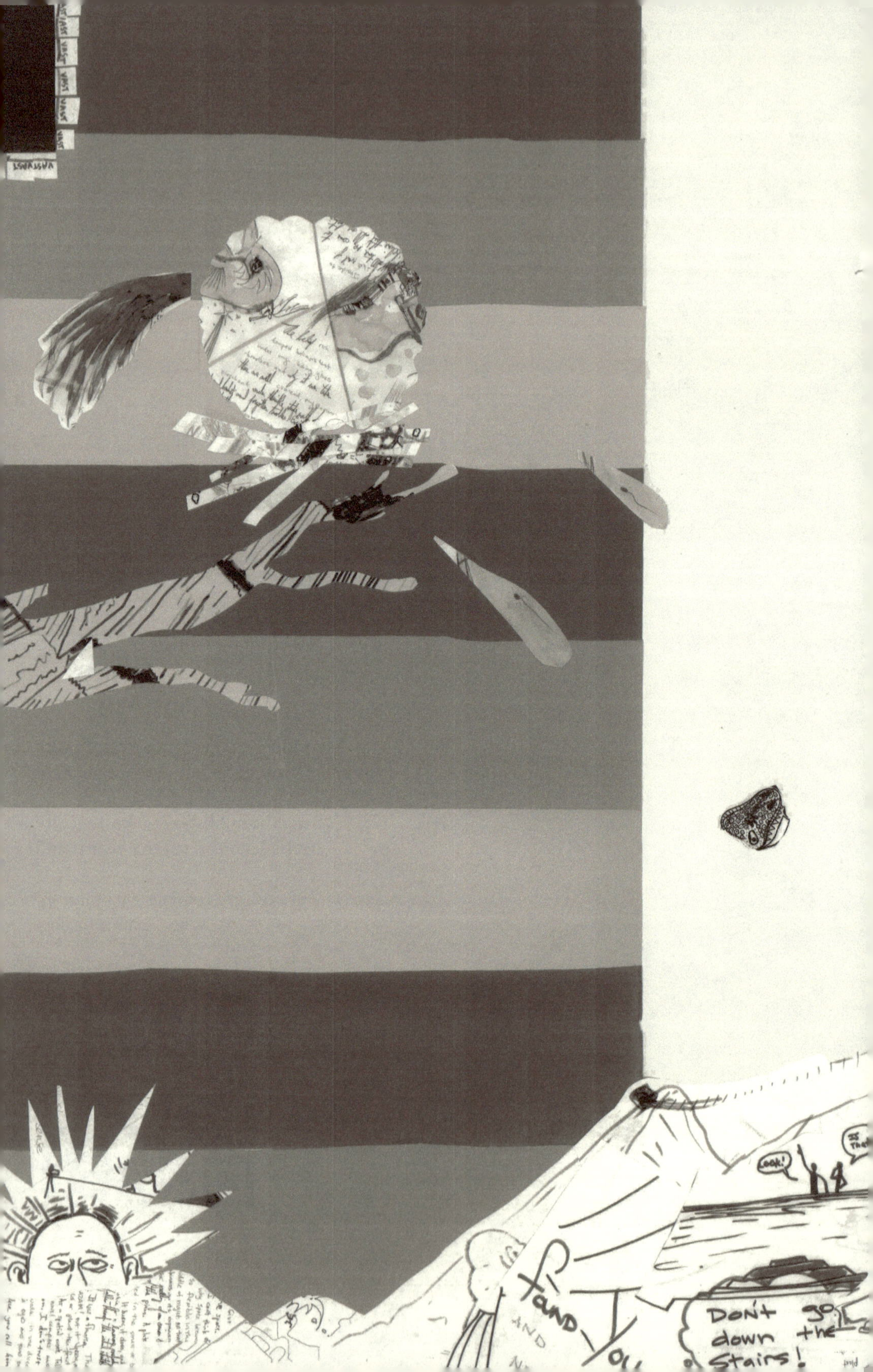
LOOK!
Don't go down the Stairs!

www.ingramcontent.com/pod-product-compliance
Lightning Source LLC
LaVergne TN
LVHW051019080826
845145LV00009B/2701
9780985518004